Holding On:
Poems on Coping with Loss after Miscarriage
By
Danielle Erwin

Copyright © 2019 Danielle Erwin.

All rights reserved. No parts of his publication may be reproduced, distributed or transmitted in any form or by any means, including photocopying, recording, or other electronic or mechanical methods, without the prior written permission of the publisher, except in the case of brief quotations embodied in critical reviews and certain other noncommercial uses permitted by copyright law.

ISBN: 978-1-674-71109-6 (Paperback)
Library of Congress Control Number: 2019920442

Any references to historical events, real people, or real places are used fictitiously. Names, characters, and places are products of the author's imagination.

Front cover image by Maya Alexandria Shoemaker for Urbanflatlays.
Book design by Tasha Morris.

Self-published by Danielle Erwin

First print edition 2019.

Printed in the United States of America

Contents

Introduction 4
Acknowledgments 6
Foreword 7
In Memory of 8
Standing in the Sorrow 9
    What Could Have Been 10
    Clinging to the Past 24
    Doubt and Denial 39
    Holding on to Hurt 45
    Ailing in Anger 49
    Steeped in Sorrow 55
Grasping for God 73
    Looking to the Future 74
    Finding Faith 84
Seeking A New Normal 126
    Seeking Sanity 131
    Challenges of Change 142
    How Miscarriages Affect Relationships 158
    Hope in Healing 166

Introduction

I carried four babies to term, and didn't think pregnancy loss would, or could, happen to me. I thought that since I love everything surrounding pregnancy, birth, and babies, that I was immune to miscarriage. I had that sort of innocence about me and I believed it would never be taken away.

In Dec 2018, I had a subchorionic bleed that never subsided. I found out I had a partial placental abruption. It was New Year's Day 2018. The next day, an ultrasound revealed that the baby wasn't growing properly. He was behind by a week or two. Two weeks later, the follow up sonogram showed that he was gone. I was induced the following day and he was born on January 17, 2018 after 19 hours and 38 minutes of labor. He was buried that afternoon. I was numb and in denial for months. Then I got pregnant with Lucy. I was a bundle of nerves, and just when nerves started to subside, so did my pregnancy nausea. One day, I suddenly felt better. My gut told me something was off, so I went to the ER. Turns out her heart rate had slowed and my hcg was through the roof. I later found out that I had a partial molar pregnancy and had to have a d&c since I wasn't passing baby on my own. Lucy Rose was buried exactly 7 months after Mark William, on Aug 17, 2018.

It wasn't until after my second miscarriage that I finally acknowledged I needed a therapist, and from sessions with her, I came to understand that denial is more than not believing something happened. In my case, I was telling the stories of my losses as if they happened to someone else. I wasn't FULLY accepting that they are my stories. MY baby saints.

We will always hold onto the memory of our baby saints and throughout our lifelong journey through grief, the emotions we feel will vary daily. What's more is we all have different ways of expressing our grief. Each emotion I have felt after miscarrying Mark and Lucy has been tied to me holding on to something, whether it be sorrow, pain, hope, faith, or what have you. The words of the poems that follow are my heartbeats on paper. Since giving birth to Mark, I have found my troubles pouring out on paper, and God's healing Love speaking time me in the same way. My hope is that these same words of mine resonate with even one grieving mother, and that the Words our Lord gave to me to help me continue on, also helps a mother seeking Love and Support in such a difficult and lonely time.

God bless, and may all our saints intercede for us that we may be with them one day in Heaven, blessed to be with our Lord and all Saints and angels forevermore.

Saints Mark William and Lucy Rose, pray for us.

Acknowledgments

I would like to thank everyone who has supported me and who continue to walk with me as I wander this road to healing, always reminding me that keeping hope through the sorrow will lead to Joy.

Foreword

I started writing poetry after I miscarried Mark and then Lucy because I found I expressed my grief better through pen. I shared them with friends who persuaded me to publish so as to help other women lost in the shadows of sadness after miscarriage. My hope is that these women will find solace and solidarity through these words, knowing they are not alone, as heart breaking as this experience is.

May God bless you, and may you know that, even when you feel utterly alone, He is there. Trust in Him always, even in your darkest hours. He is your guiding Light and He will lead you through as He does for me although it may not look as you want it to. The peace you seek may at once be the tangible peace and comfort that is offered on earth. But the peace you seek is not the temporary peace of the earth, which is fleeting. Seek His Peace, remembering that whatever happens here on earth is drawing you closer to Him. May that hope bring you everlasting Joy through this deep sorrow.

In Memory of Mark William and Lucy Rose Erwin,

Born 1/17/18 and 8/15/18

Standing in the Sorrow

What Could Have Been

Today (1/31/18)

There have been plenty of times when something I have seen or done reminded me of Marky, no matter how well I think I'm doing or how far I think I have come in the healing process, it is sometimes enough to take me back. And so, I have come to realize that grief is not linear.

I put bottles and the Bumbo away
Thinking back to two weeks ago, today
I wear a bittersweet smile
Won't be using those for a while
I know he's in a better place
Still a tear rolls down my face
I think of what could have been
My thoughts return to Heaven again
There will always be a missing part
Remembered love with every beat of my heart
A short life lived and quickly gone Above
A short life, but one no less loved.

Due Date (6/15/2018)
(Marky was due today)

Another anniversary. I just finished my doula training the day before. I had healed to the point where I was ready for that, and I was ready to be a birth doula. To attend births and support mamas and families. I couldn't wait, but I could still recall the day he was born and the day he was due. It will always be in my mind.

On this day, you were due
Only God has carried me through
These past 5 months without you
Inside

I've felt an emptiness within
A hole where you should have been
Where babies til 40 weeks end
Abide

Five months have passed and still
I remember snow outside the window sill
Coldest day of my life it will
Remain

It was cold the day we met you
The warmth of your soul passed through
So I did what I had to do and would do
Again

You were born sleeping and
I, for a moment, held my heart in my hand
You'd gone to that faraway Land
of Heaven

Every day, you pass through my mind
We buried you, left your body behind
I can't let you go, I struggle and find,
Child Seven

I've had to find a new way
To live, keeping emotions at bay
Unsure of what others would think and say
Of me

Just keep on, act as if you're not
Grieving, parent the ones you've got
Forget this battle you've fought,
This memory

But how could I let go
For all of my children, I know
Even if your life does not show
On earth

On earth My love for you carries a pain
Seeking to hold you, I strain
To get closer to Heaven through your gain,
Your berth

I rarely stop and think of how low
I feel, daily through the motions I go
Never able to just think or take it slow
Any day

I struggle to put a smile on my face
I go through the motions by God's Grace
Marky's brief life is a mem'ry to embrace
Always

No matter how hard I try
Regardless of the tears I cry
With every word I write
I keep trying to fight
But No matter how short or long
I can't write your memory away with a song

Footprints on My Heart (10/3/18)

These daily reminders of what is missing enter my life uninvited, often blindsiding me. It's quite cumbersome to keep these in my heart, while at the same time welcoming my suffering, and allowing God to work through it all.

You left your footprints on my heart
Though we both be worlds apart
I can't hear yours beat
But having you in Heaven's more sweet

I can't physically hold you in my arms
Nor hear you or see your smiling charm
I walk daily feeling your loss as pain
My body forgetting your eternal gain

Breathing isn't easy anymore
Never know what each day has in store
My body wants naught but to stay in place
And to behold your baby face

To return to moments with your life here
Enjoy my pregnancy without death's fear
Those final moments before you left
When the ultrasound made me bereft

Disbelief but knowing it's all real
Losing all I ever seemed to feel
All within me seemed to leave
To earthly hope I tried to cleave

Your ways are not mine, O Lord
They're greater than deaths piercing sword
This month renew my fearless bound'ry
Help me proudly carry this stone around me

The desire and hope I have in You
Is not just that Your Grace carry me through
But that increase with each pain I feel within
Desire to see my saints further me from sin

Rest in Peace (10/17/18)

I go back...
St. Mark William (Marky) and St. Lucy Rose, pray for me.
Marky- born and buried Jan 17th, 2018 and Lucy- born Aug 15th, buried Aug 17th near her brother.

Forever missed,
Forever loved
I want them back,
But they dwell Above.

In my heart ev'ry day
On my mind forever
I pray one day
We'll be together

I hope to see them again
And I shall not cease
To speak of them
Til we all Rest In Peace

Wish You Back (10/27/18)

Sometimes it feels like I'm trapped in an unending nightmare, one which I wish to begin the story again and choose my own ending. Alas, here I am, wishing I could wish you back.

Someone wake me
I'm ready to be done with this
Why can't this let me be
It's something I won't miss

Yet I cling to every piece
For its part of your memory
Grief is part of this lease
I seek to keep what can no longer be

Send away the sorrow
Keep you here instead
But life is something we borrow
We're here on God's time, then we're dead

Something hard to grasp
I can't seem to understand
Why is grief what I clasp
And not a baby's hand

I dwell in an opposite world
Holding onto earthly pain
In each moment that unfurls
Looking on with disdain

Knowing heaven is where they dwell
Wishing heaven and earth could unite
Reminded of empty arms, tears swell
The coldness of the emptiness bites

Knowing what I cannot have again
Reminded daily of what I lack
Wish to go back to where I've been
If only I could wish you back

Breathless (11/3/18)

Longing for more than their memories to be with me, it's as if I keep waiting for it to happen on this earth, only to remember I won't see them again 'til my time here is done, if I do it well, 'til He calls me Home, 'til the day I become breathless.

Breathless, I breathe
Inside, I seethe
My stomach is stuck
Feel hit by a truck

Days take longer
They make me stronger
Much darker at night
My heart loses sight

Weeks pass by slowly
New normal comes closer to me
Ready to move on
Make the past all gone

Constantly try to climb
Mountains in my mind
Reach the top
But again I drop

Cling to each minute
Like it's the last with you in it
Inhale so slow
Reluctant to let go

Pretend I'm in control
But God has your soul
I can't bring you back
Prayer doesn't work like that

Realize how lowly I am
A servant of the Lamb
I wish with ev'ry thought
But realize it's all for naught

This life feels like a dream
Your memories burst at the seam
Even when I let go and breathe
Your memories refuse to leave

I can emerge from this rain
Only their mem'ry will remain
Know that my heart will be restless
Til the day I become breathless

Dragging On (11/5/18)

It feels like this will take forever. This grief, this desire for my two saints to be here with me. They are my children, and like those I have here with me they will never be forgotten. I will remember them every day. So yes, this will drag on the rest of my life. I will not forget a moment with them in it. The thought of them not can drag me down. But I can also choose to allow it to bring me, up closer to them. So I keep them in my daily thoughts and prayers, and they are present in this life, as it appears to merely be dragging on.

3 months ago today
The feeling never goes away
The last beats of her heart
Death made us worlds apart

My entire self recalls
Walking out from the halls
That emptiness returns
My whole being yearns

Wish to see her again
Though she's always within
I still want one more chance
Just one more glance

Her body so tiny
Her soul so shiny
Perfect and pain-free
She resides in Heaven above me

Still doesn't human feelings erase
Nor the desire to see her 40 week face
Lying perfect and alive in my arms
But at 8 weeks she left the place so warm

And today those thoughts rush back
She's here, though her presence lack
She comes through the emotions and tears
So this is how it will be the rest of my years

The memories continue dragging on
Ones I wouldn't wish to see gone
She, like her brother before
Engrained in my heart forevermore

The Firsts (12/14/18)

This Christmas we will see
Empty spaces beside the tree
Where you would be sitting
Beside your dad and me

Presents with your name
No toys, nor game
Just something to remember you
And render my tears untamed

In a room that's full of joy
Your siblings unwrap each toy
I take and hold both of yours
And picture of a saint girl and boy

I can only think of what you'd do
If you unwrapped the presents here for you
They'd not be pictures of your namesake
But toys, books, whatever your sister drew

I sit like I did last year
Feeling empty and full of fear
Knowing something's amiss
Now I know I was losing someone dear

The coming year's supposed to be better
From my chains, I come unfettered
Instead I sit here feeling all emotions
And writing this poetic letter

And I feel forever bound
Not sure I'll feel better each new round
I feel like I'm returning and then
My heart for you two begins to pound

So on this anniversary, I'll thirst
Each one has continued to hurt
So they've done with each loss
But neither so much as the firsts

First Christmas (12/25/18)

I try so hard to fake it til I make it, but that never works. I sit here on the first Christmas without both of you, watching all things unfold as they've done in years past, but this time with a new lens. And once more, instead of seeking comfort from this earth, realizing God is always reliable, always there to listen to our troubles, and send comfort in His Spirit, comfort unlike any we would feel on this earth.

I force a smile of joy
As the kids unwrap each toy
On the day the Saviour is born
This silent Christmas morn

Thinkin if I can fake it
Pretend to be just fine
I'll eventually make it
And my life will be back to mine

Yet with each subsequent smile
The hole grows bigger within
As if the thousands of miles
Aren't reminders of what's been

The reminders of love
The prayers and hugs from friends
Examples of those Above
Of what I should be til the end

Empathetic hug to a struggling soul
Who's trying to mend her heart
Is what helps to make her whole
When it's doing its best to fall apart

Just being with someone
Is what a person needs
A hug when she feels done
Permission for her heart to bleed

So as I walk through my day
In rough waters wading
I feel joy my way
After the time of waiting

On this first Christmas without
You celebrating, too
I believe without a doubt
Hope through sorrow yields joy anew

What If (9/29/19)

Goin' through life with every thought
Wonderin' if I'm livin' as I ought
Tryin' to just soak it all in
Slow myself down from this tailspin
Tryin' to get Where you are
Hard to believe I've made it this far

Sometimes I can't help but wonder what if
What if I still had you
What would we be goin' through
What would my days look like
What if we still had the night
I'll be thinkin' bout it 'til I'm stiff
I'm gonna be wonderin' what if

Balancing life where I am at
One little move and then I'm back
Every situation I've been in
Has left me sittin' there, wonderin'...

Wonderin' what if
What if I still had you
What would we be goin' through
What would my days look like
What if we still had the night
I'll be thinkin' bout it 'til I'm stiff
I'm gonna be wonderin' what if

Thankin' God for all He's given me under the stars
Thankin' God for giving you a Space Above the stars

Still I'm caught wonderin' what if
What if I still had you
What would we be goin' through
What would my days look like
What if we still had the night
I'll be thinkin' bout it 'til I'm stiff
I'm gonna be wonderin' what if

Clinging to the Past

Anniversaries (10/17/2018)

I often find myself thinking I'm on the road to healing, as if it's some finite thing, then something like an anniversary will come up, and I'm set back, or reminded rather of where I really am on this journey of healing.

I walk around like a ghost
Think of them and I'm toast
I'd start the day off in the clear
Remember the date, I'm back here

I shrink from what I used to be
When resurfaces their memory
I lost, I birthed, I buried
Covered the box then scurried

They return every day
Their love doesn't stray
On certain days especially
Of their story they remind me

I'm reminded of their heavenly presence
Their former earthly existence
The story of their lives returned
A mere date their mem'ry spurned

My feet firm on the ground
Free from that which I was bound
Til the days come round to me
Those days, their departure's anniversary

Sleepless (12/10/18)

There are nights that find me sleepless, and those nights I wonder how I'll make it through the next day not letting my exhaustion negatively affect those around me. It's not simple and sometimes my body remains awake, thinking about them, but I ask for their intercession and my day goes smoothly. They're there to remind me He is in control, even when my nights are sleepless.

Dark of night surrounds me
Nothing here to ground me
From sleep my body takes flight
Close my eyes at dawns breaking light

The minutes tick by
The night did fly
But when day arrives
I'll struggle to thrive

Pulling through each hour
At the pace of a budding flower
Patiently awaiting the help of the Son
To finish what's set to be done

To do all things with grace
Each with a smile upon my face
To not give in
To vice's sin

To treat all with kindness
To treat my exhaustion with blindness
To know that this day won't last
Like the rest, this too shall pass

Letting Go (12/22/18)

I remember back almost a year ago when all was set in motion, I stare at the wall, like it's blocking me from seeing beyond the sorrow. I try to look through it to see the other end, the other Side, the place where my saints reside. And I know neither of us will ever be letting go.

It's been a year
I shed a tear
Remember being alone in that room
With the quiet stillness in my womb
From the beginning something was wrong
In my heart I knew it all along
Like God had been preparing me
For where you were soon to be
Somehow I seemed to know
All that time, my body was letting go

Your heart stopped here on earth
And to your body I gave birth
Now, I stare at the clock
Time ticking off
Trying to look beyond the wall
To see the purpose of it all
Try to see through to the other side
That place where my saints reside
It helps me to know
None of us are letting go

The pictures of our family hang
Missing two of our little gang
The empty parts indicate
You've gone beyond the Gate
With all the saints and angels, you
Do what all heavenly creatures do
Pray for those you know
Are holding on, never letting go

Live It Again (12/22/18)

Tomorrow is the anniversary of the sub chorionic bleed that led to the partial placental abruption that led to losing Marky. So it begins and so I'll relive it. It's my grief, my process, and that's ok.

The sadness stays here
The memory remains
Pierced with a spear
I Remember the pains
Millions of thoughts in my head
But none of them are words
A flurry of emotions in their stead
The anniversary attacks me like swords
I knew it was coming
I wasn't trying to hide
I wasn't caught running
From the storm swelling inside
I wanted to commemorate
The short life that you had
I knew the sorrow would reverberate
Never thought it'd be so bad
I lie here in bed curled in a ball
For tomorrow I wait
I know I'll relive it all
I know to anticipate
So much to relive
So much to recall
So much did you give
So much to us all

Then when you left
And it felt worse than before
Now I am bereft
And shake to the core
I return to my knees
Once more humbled
I'm sure everyone will see
Me as I crumble
And it's all okay
I'm gonna live it again
It's not for anyone to say
How to move forward and when

Here I Go Again (12/23/18)

It may be difficult to find someone to talk to, someone who truly understands, and in those moments, I have turned to prayer, for no One knows better this sorrow than He Who died for us on the Cross. He will help us carry ours if only we ask.

Breath caught within
Seeking to be let out
Like some mortal sin
One doesn't talk about

Tryin to find
The right person around
To speak my mind
Release what's been bound

A priest for my soul
To relinquish my broken heart
To help me unroll
What's been tearing me apart

Memories of losses so painful
Hold me hostage inside
To most, talk of which is disdainful
Most push that memory aside

To the High Priest I turn
He Who knows this too well
I know my heart He won't spurn
As the memories begin to swell

My body and mind recall
Now's different than then
I relive the memory of it all
Here I go again

The Last Day (12/31/18)

Remembering Marky's last day. It was January 2nd, 2018 when I had my appointment for a sonogram, the last time I saw him alive. And now I hope to be with him and his sister with our Lord in Heaven on my last day.

Got up that mornin'
Knew something was wrong
You weren't gonna be
Around for very long

At my appointment
We tried to hope
Looking back now
It was a way to cope

We did all we could
To keep you around
But you were done
And soon, Heaven-bound

Didn't know for sure
And I didn't dare say
In case there was a chance
It wasn't the last day

Two weeks later
That feeling remained
The thoughts wouldn't disappear
They'd become engrained

Nothing felt different
Than the appointment before
And my fears were confirmed
You were here no more

The picture didn't lie
And I stared in disbelief
You were no longer moving
You remained still on the screen

Now, I knew for sure
But just couldn't say
There was no more chance
And this was your last day

Things were set into motion
A labor of love
So I could deliver your body
Though your soul dwelt Above

On the second day
You were born
Buried in the afternoon
After coming early that morn

A beautiful little boy
I held and stared at you
So tiny and so fragile
Nothing more I could do

I saw for sure
And the proof there lay
One more chance to see you
On this last day

This is not the end
For we fully believe
That we shall meet again
If my soul our Lord receives

If I may live to be pure
In what I do and say
I pray for the chance to meet you
On my last day

A Day to Remember (1/16/18)

It's been a year. Yesterday since the sonogram revealed Marky had passed. Today since the induction began. And tomorrow since he was born and buried. And this year I'm working on a book with mine and my saints' stories. It'll include all the poetry.

So today I recall heading into the hospital to be induced
To deliver the little saint's body which earthly life it refused.
I remember the labor of that day
Which for me began promptly at eight.
19hrs 38 minutes later you came
A few hours after, you had your saintly name.
Later that day we left
Carrying you to your grave bereft.
What started going downhill in December
Lead us to a day we will always remember.
You never made it to our home
And on this earth you shall not roam
Here my thoughts of longing once again
Are directed towards the King of men
Who has, the sadness in my heart
Continuously bid depart
All the while my heart shan't cease
Holding on to what it should release
It knows only with your grace
And looking longingly upon your face
This suffering it doth not despise
Nor the merciful gaze from Your eyes
As it struggles to trust in Your love
And remain focused on You Above

Laying at Your feet earthly pain
Mulling constantly o'er Your Heavenly gain
Laying all its sorrow to rest
Dwelling on your eternal conquest
Trying hard Your soothing Voice to hear
For merely listening will relieve my fear
After calming my heart's earthly distress
Change its sorrow to Your Joyous Happiness
A saint made starting in September
Makes this earthly loss a day to remember

A Year (on 1/17/19)

And the day after the induction began...I remember that frigid day, sitting on the bench in the cemetery, holding tight to one of my children during the burial rite. Aware, but in total denial, of what was going on.

It's been a year
Since you left your Mark
You're no longer here
But I still feel your spark

As I prepared for today
I have realized
That which I celebrate
Is for but my earthly eyes

You're not sitting beside me
While you stare at lights on a cake
The true Light of Heaven you see
Where Joy you don't have to make

Th'Eternal Feast is already prepared
No counting your years in exile
I rejoice in that time you were spared
And pray all here might join you after a while

St. Marky, pray for us.

The Me I Used to Know (1/31/19)

After my losses, I can't go back to the me I used to know.

I never used to be
Able to confine a joke within me
I'd sing whatever song came to mind
Now I've left that all behind
It seems every shower time
I touch emotions with my rhyme
Once a year passed, I'd never fear to go
Explore the heart of the me I used to know

I used to find joy and keep up with the game
Of life and most any sport you name
Handling everything that came my way
With ease of a mind that never strayed
Felt confident in my doula passion
Ready to follow my true birthie passion
Until once upon a year ago
I abandoned the me I used to know

My arms weren't full of lead
Many thoughts raced through my head
I was devoid of this emptiness
Never thought I'd have babies to miss
Fun me rushed through my veins
Where now the numbness reigns
Those roads I never feared to go
Belong to the me I used to know

My body never felt so dead
It was easier to get out of bed
Looked forward to each day
Laughed at funnies my kids would say
Was always quick with wit
Now it tends to take a little bit
My mind seems now to go
Stuck with the me I used to know

Tried not to shy from God's Will
I find myself hiding still
As if in the Garden, clothed, ashamed
Hesitant to come when He calls my name
To find out what it means to answer His call
After taking and refusing to leave last year's fall
Afraid to now spring and go
Try out the new version of the me I used to know

Marky's Memorial Mass (6/15/19)

The priest walks in
The faithful gatherin'
To hear words so wise

Raw and real
Can't hide my feels
So speak my eyes

Your name was spoken
My heart re-broken
In but a second's time

With angel choirs singing
Bells at Consecration ringing
Just past the Church bell's chime

You're with me again
Like you were then
But even closer inside

With you in Heaven's heart
You continue to do your part
Til I with you once more reside

Now come the tears
Ending the year
I'm human and weak

You're still gone
Emotions hold on
Peace I continue to seek

My sweet Marky, know this
You and Lucy taught me bliss
Is not found in this place

But rather, I've learned
That when comes my turn
I'll find Peace in God's Face

He sent His Son
And victory, He won
Over the sting of death

So bring me closer each Mass
Til I'm There, at last
Upon my dying breath

Doubt and Denial

The Burial (9/15/18)

With my husband and kids and friends gathered round, I could barely utter a coherent sound. During the burial rite I whispered lest I cry. But goofed around as I lowered them down. Joked with my kids about playing in dirt, wondered why I didn't feel sad and hurt. It was in this time, all it would take was a touch, or a word, and I would have been drawn back to reality, I would have been in touch with what was happening.

My world is upside down
I may seem like a clown
Nothing seems real
Shock is what I feel

You see me smile
You wonder all the while
Where are my tears
Why aren't they here

This is no time to joke
Why can't I be serious like other folk
Like I just don't understand
The serious time at hand

You wonder why I don't cry
Why my emotional responses are awry
My façade is strong
Though it seems so wrong

This should be grief,
My joy robbed by a thief,
Happiness taking a break,
But I think it's all a mistake

Like this box I bury isn't mine
Pile on the dirt, and I'll be fine
Everything settles like the dust
Return to life as I must

Looking back on each time
Amidst the sorrow, I was sublime
Yet afterwards the rain would fall
Winds would blow, and sorrow call

Yet everyone else had moved on
Solemn faces from that day were gone
Both times I missed my chance
To join with others in the dance

My tears came too late for me
When together with everyone, I would be
I was numb, then, and so
After that day, their emotions would go

Since then I've been like a lonely tree
Standing against the force from the sea
Expected to return to my norm
Left alone to weather the storm

Why did I have to seem so tame
Why can't everyone's feelings be the same
It appeared I didn't comprehend
So the wrong message I did send

How I wish our emotions would align
Or that somehow you'd see a sign
Stages of grief are in disarray
So they shouldn't be arranged that way

The Unknown (2/7/19)

It's as if I've been dissociating from the experience and telling the story of my losses as if it's someone else's story. I tell the facts and leave out the painful recollection, the emotions buried.

I put a piece of my
Broken heart on a shelf
Turned away and now I'm
Worlds apart from myself
Wandering mindlessly through
The halls of this place I call home
Even amidst those who know me, I remain so alone

They can't say
They've been to this place
Where I'm currently stuck
Putting on my poker face
They haven't traveled the road
That leads to the stone
This place remains to them

The untraveled unknown
I hide from my thoughts
That lead to sadness
Try to cover it up
With a façade of gladness
Unsuccessfully coast through
Each tiresome day
Wishing I could get in touch with

The me I've kept at bay
From the ties that bind
I remain aloof
Refusing to touch the past
Is all I need for proof
The pain of loss too deep
My hiding sets the tone
For fear is that which keeps
Me from traveling to the unknown

I try to reunite the parts of me
Everything I once was
But they don't fit together
And that's all because
Part of that me was you
Safely dwelling within me
And that is now something
That's no more to be

The memory of that moment
When they said you're gone
They couldn't find a heartbeat
And I laid there alone
You weren't moving on the screen
I can't find a heartbeat hon
The words that drained life from me
Are unexplored in the unknown

So I lie helplessly here
Understanding this is the moment when
After Regaining my composure
I knew I wouldn't be me again
It's the one moment left to explore
While the rest of me has grown
But refrained from flourishing because
I need to unite it with the unknown

A pleading mind I had
In those minutes leading to
The words that stuck forever
Words I can't undo
As all feeling drained from
My head to my toes
I tried to brush them off
Thinking this is how life goes

I can't stop life for this
There are things I must do
And so I pushed that moment
Tucked deep in my heart with you
Thought eventually I would
Set a different tone
I couldn't bring you back
From the Glorious Unknown

I lack that sort of power
It's not a part of me
Yet I wish to unhear those words
As if in my arms you'd be
Like if I just walk through my day
I'll eventually wake from this
And in my arms will be
A baby and all the bliss

At each day's end I realize
That not to be with you
And I fall asleep knowing
The sonographers words were true
Replaying that moment again and again
Not that it reverses what's done
Hoping It would help me feel what I should
Become acquainted with the unknow

Say It Isn't So (9/29/19)

Remembering them and their stories today and always.

Walk into the room
Somehow they all know
They're all filled with gloom
Had a hunch it was your time to go

This image on the screen
It can't possibly be
Why're you lying there so still
You've not lived your fill
You had a lifetime to go
So say it isn't so

I'm back the very next day
Waiting for you to come
So sorry it ended this way
It was your time to go Home

You're so little in front of me
This can't possibly be
Why're you lying there so still
You've not lived your fill
I'm here holdin' onto Hope
Waiting for them to say it isn't so

In denial this moment is true
I fear letting go of you

Your image on my every heartbeat
Your picture remains inside of me
You reside in me still
In a way you always will
Holdin' a piece of Heaven ain't lettin' go
So don't say it isn't so

Holding on to Hurt

Unmendable Broken Heart (3/20/19)

Unlike a bad test score
Unfathomably hard core
This knife dug deep
The price ain't cheap
What's gone can't come back
What's gone I forever lack
My stomach in knots
This will hurt lots
Because after a bad test
I could improve the rest
But death splits apart
Unmendable broken heart

In an instant I had you here
In another instant you disappeared
I'm left to flashbacks of what woulda been
Wanting it to happen now instead of then
Why couldn't you stay safe inside of me
That place where babies are supposed to be
Here on your due date it hits me hard
Worse than the losing lottery card
Like the numbers dealt to me
Why was your life here not meant to be
I'm left here without you, splitting apart
With an Unmendable broken heart

Babies aren't supposed to leave
Even though they go where I believe
It's better all-around to be
Better than inside of me
Tagging and landing on home base
In Heaven, and the last I saw your face
Eyes closed and heartbeat erased
After I dilated and effaced
Like a typical labor for someone new

Entering this world like the morning dew
The image I have splits me apart
Leaving me with an unmendable broken heart

You left me here on my own
Your body remains, your spirit flown
Expecting me to just continue on
To push on through life with you gone
As if I could just move onto what's next
When life and death leave me perplexed

How can I just move to something new
Or walk another step without holding you
I can't think of the first thing to do
It was all supposed to be done with you
Your death is breaking me apart
With my unmendable broken heart

Melt on the floor into a puddle
My life's plan and thoughts are muddled
What did I do to this deserve
When others I seek to serve
Through their labor and delivery
My life's now shown death to me
Why make me feel insane
Disorganized thoughts of my brain
What am I to do with that I love
That gift I know came from You, Above
Why'd You build a dream to just tear apart
Into an unmendable broken heart

I know time is to heal this hurt
But why must it treat me like dirt
Why is time taking so long
Doesn't it know it doesn't belong
When this is the road I'm to travel
Why doesn't time's lengthy thread unravel
It punishes me here instead
By waiting inside my head

Making me sit and wonder
Why this dream feels asunder
When I am sitting here torn apart
Trying to mend my broken heart

So hurry and let me soar
Rekindle the flame and hear it roar
Let me wait no longer
Lord make me stronger
So I might serve all You give to me
To be who You wish me to be
A wife, mom, and doula set on course
To look back with no remorse
To tend to those falling apart
Help make whole their longing hearts

There And Back Again (7/20/19)

The day I knew you were gone
I felt so alone
Can't take back the words that were said
No heartbeat, you were dead
Felt the life drain from me
You left me hurtin, don't you see

I'll think I've moved on enough
On top of the world, I stand tough
I have those days I think I'm fine and then
I go there and back again

Down the road
Gets better, I'm told
Feelings and your memory come and go
Grief ebbs and flows

I'll think I've moved on enough
On top of the world, I stand tough
I have those days I think I'm fine and then
I go there and back again

Ailing in Anger

Your Disgruntled Servant 10/1/18

Lord I'm angry and hurt
Why did you create them from dirt
Then take them again away
This seems child's play

Tormenting my feeble heart
Tearing my life apart
It's hard to handle my losses
Why'd you give me these crosses?

I feel stuck
Emotions run amuck
I can't feel Your Grace
To help me out of this place

Why do this to me?
Where lies Your mercy?
I fail to see your plan
I'm trying all I can

My joy in life falls short
I place the ball in Your court
I'm like a toddler to this day
Finding difficulty knowing what to say

Why did you ask me to be your Job?
When I can barely handle this load
Why with You by my side
Do I seem to barely get by?

I don't seek to offend you
But I don't know what else to do
Other than to be angry and hurt
That You fashioned and returned both soon to dirt

To my hCG levels after my partial molar pregnancy with Lucy (10/5/18)

She's gone,
So why are you still holding on?
My womb is bare
So why are you still there?
Get out of me
A place you shouldn't be
You shouldn't grieve
You never did believe
Why're you in denial?
This was never your trial
You're no hero
Why can't you just fall to zero?
You're nothing anymore
So it's time to walk out the door
And next time
Don't commit this crime
Behave when you rise again,
When you come, make amends

The Journey (10/5/18)

I write but don't have all the words
My soul's pierced with a thousand swords
This emotion's a pest
Pent up in my tightened chest
Locked up and no more key
Anger remains slowly killing me

I don't know how to properly dispose
Grief's grip won't let go
Those I love are caught in the fight
Between my soul and it's dark night
My loss is not their crime
Yet they're stuck doing the time

I remain in this place
Emotions taking up space
My brain takes on the task
Of putting on my body's mask
It's fight or flight
Cuz something ain't right

My heart can't find the right beat
Rhythm takes a back seat

My system is unplugged
My function is rugged
A short has been detected
So I shut down to remain protected

I live in this sunset paradise
Lingering dusk wearing down my eyes
The end is constantly in sight
I hold on with all my might
Just out of reach is the moon
This flicker of light my only boon

The promise of the new day's dawn
When the orb's light is gone
Yet for now I remain in its gaze
Awaiting my new beginning's rays
Being taken through life sick on a gurney
Learning to be happy on this journey

Our life will not be the heavenly joy
That thought is the devils ploy
We aren't promised final happiness here
We're called to live troubles without fear
To live knowing Christ is close by
Remembering his yoke put our burdens nigh

My Choice (11/1/18)

The guilt, the anger, the shame. I felt it. You know those times you may not have been planning a pregnancy, but yet in marriage, one promise to God is your openness to life? And when you are open to life and have feelings of anything but excitement upon seeing those two pink lines then that baby is gone…you feel guilty. Wondering if you did something to make this happen. Angry at God for allowing it. Shame for even wishing things were different.

I think back to
How two in a row have died
Wonder what did I do
Blame myself til I cried

Angry at myself, how I felt
Openness to Life was all for naught
Dealing with the hand I was dealt
No one else at fault

It's so final, You're gone
Having no life or voice
Makes me think I've done wrong
But this loss wasn't my choice

Navigating the memories as I grieve
Conflicted reaction to two lines
Hard to accept and believe
Your deaths weren't from the Divine

Wasn't my choice for you to leave
Though my anxiety was so high
Losing you, briefly my minds reprieve
Forever afraid I let you die

Why did you go when
It wasn't my choice to lose you
Felt guilty as sin
I didn't really want you to

I ask all these questions of me
But it isn't really fair
When all life belongs to He
When my cross He does bare

I think sustaining life is completely my role
But life belongs to the Omniscient
I think I know it all, I spin out of control
When I think the choice is my burden

I continue dwelling in anguish
Thinking the choice was mine to make
I can't continue like this
As if their lives were mine to take

So hard to resist the hellish foe
Thoughts the faults were mine
So hard to let it go
Into the control of the Divine

Blame remains stuck in my mind
If these words I type would set me free
Praying He heals my heart, pained and blind
My choice it would be

Steeped in Sorrow

Imprints (9/5/18)

It really is a struggle. Three weeks since my d & c and Lucy's burial, the weakness comes along. I felt fine until after the burials of both, her and her brother. I came to understand that I was in denial. Then it hit me in moments of the days following. All I have left are memories as the imprints of my little saints.

Three weeks ago today
My heart still can't utter a word
I have so much to say
But sadness is all that's heard

Words are trapped inside
Like a babe who cannot speak
I'm just along for the daily ride
Keeping the pace, though I am weak

My heart lies alone
Hiding like my words in the dark
Where innocent light once shone
Are now imprints of my Lucy and my Mark

Uninvited Guest (10/5/18)

My hCG levels rose, reminding me again of what had happened that caused them to skyrocket to abnormal levels in the first place. Although they dropped the following week, it was as if they wanted to remind me again of why they were being monitored in the first place.

Knockin' on the door
Ain't her style
It was me she came for
First time in a while
Couldn't bear to leave
Me well enough alone
She had to return
Hang around my neck like a stone
She wouldn't depart
At my behest
She lingered in my heart
The uninvited guest

Memory Returned to Me (10/21/18)

I was putting baby things away in the storage room and was tempted to give them away because seeing everything I wasn't using lead to your memory being returned to me in full.

I walked down the stairs today
Bearing words I cannot say
To the ones who dwell as saints
In that dwelling Place so quaint

Clinging with a grip of death
Holding on with every breath
To the things I now relinquish
Meant for those lives extinguished

Stoically I descend to a place
Where I can wear my solemn face
I move beyond the door
Where belongings are in store

Slowly my heavy feet encroach
What my hurting heart must approach
Once more reopening the wound
Seeing their memories so soon

I know what I must do
And I shan't falter to carry through
Open their boxes of mem'ries I must
Their name cards I hurriedly thrust

Once those and other items are in
I close their boxes hurriedly like I sinned
To the shelf they're returned
Forever their mem'ries are burned

I stand back on the brink of tears
Stare at what's left of my dears
Reason with myself
Not to clear stuff from the shelf

For more in various places remain
Treasured items I peer at with disdain
As if they committed some crime
Now mistaken traitors of their time

When they proved helpful once before
I tossed them to keep them in store
Yet every time I see them there reside
Overwhelming torrent rears up inside

So now the task befalls my heart
To make these things dearly depart
As some others are put away
These here aren't meant to stay

Regret in the future I might
This tiny hand's slight
But in order that the future come to be
The present task's completion I must see.

Sitting with Grief (10/22/18)

Emotionally drained
Mentally strained
Like I'm hit by a train
I go against the grain

Wake every morn
Heart struck with a thorn
Hard to rise from bed
You're mem'ry in my head

Struggle to rise
Heavy my eyes
Easier to stay
I drag through the day

Others depend
Days without end
They need me to just be
Oh, why can't they see?

I need a break
How long will it take?
No end in sight
Endless night

Envelopes my heart
Don't know where to start
In a rush to heal
It's hard to be real

Wish for my former life
Innocent mother and a wife
Struggle to accept
This "new normal" concept

I move forward with a fight
Trying to decide what's right
What is too much?
What can't I touch?

They say to take my time
It's not a predictable line
Healing doesn't mean
Your loss can't be seen

That's not what it's about
Let the tears flow out
Others don't need to approve
The way your heart moves
It's not about them
They didn't lose their gem
They don't make your call
Their back's not against the wall

So feel without holding back
Struggle to accept what you lack
Sit with the heavy morn
Dispose your mind of their scorn

It's not theirs to feel
Don't forget you're real
Don't listen to them tease
Carry on as you please

So sit with your grief
Don't allow any thief
To have any say
Or tell you not to feel that way

Broken Down (10/25/18)

Grief paralyzes you. You are stuck in memory of your loss. It's so hard to rise out of it, but all important not to rush it. Remember relief of sorts will come on its own time. Even though you feel you'll be stuck like a car on the side of the road broken down.

I sit unable to move
Unchanged by the wheels of time
Fitting nicely in each groove
Gears turn by me without blinking an eye

I'm at a standstill with my own clock
Like an unending duel
It smirks at me with its relentless tick tock
Laughing at my unending pain so cruel

The world goes round
But I can't go with it
To self-made chains I am bound
And with my loss, alone I sit

Force the smile
Fake it til I make me new
Trudging that extra mile
Not sure what to do

Try to forget about my limit
I must be boundless now
I feel I'm unfit
To let my feelings show

And when night is here
I feel alone
Just me and my fear
My hurt and my unknown

No one knows the extent
Of what I need to heal
Of the trauma I underwent
To them it's not as real

The losses engrained so deep
And I can't completely say
How much the consequences I now reap
Affect me in every way

Here I lie like never before
Thoughts of their deaths so dark
Desiring to be much more
Than this shadow of myself so stark
My face isn't what used to be mine
What others have known through the years
My eyes have lost their shine
As they release their tears

Thin black veil over me
Shrouded by a burial gown
I'm not what I used to be
I'm on the side of life's road, broken down

Bittersweet (11/11/18)

In every moment during my labor with Mark and my D&C with Lucy, and those moments thereafter, and although I was in denial of my miscarriages, I wanted to remain in the time and places, to never lose sight, to never let go, though the moments weren't those of happiness, but rather bittersweet.

Bittersweet the moment
The hour, the time
Bittersweet the minute
I hear the chime
Bittersweet it is
When you come out from inside
Bittersweet holding you
Though your heartbeat has died
Bittersweet the pain and joy
That fall in my tears' shine
Bittersweet the realization
In Heaven, saints you are mine

Bittersweet pain, I labored
But at the same time was numb
Bittersweet moments I gazed upon you
And to denial I succumbed
Bittersweet shock, I buried you
Supported by those surrounding me
Bittersweet to see their solemn faces
They were there where I couldn't be
Bittersweet silence we departed
All returned to their reality
Bittersweet life to which I returned
And suffer bittersweet sorrow silently

Free Flow (12/4/18)

There is joy for knowing, but pain and sorrow freely flowing.
And that's ok.

It's 4 o'clock and lonely here
Thoughts of you won't disappear
I've done all that I can do
This, and every day to make it through
Every time, I begin and end the same
My life revolves around your names
The pit grows bigger within
Held, like you were, inside my skin
No way out, it continues to ache
Won't release for my heart's sake
That once full part of my soul
Is now the darkest hole
Winds blow from my storm's eye
Hurricane rains become my cry
The heavy emptiness remains
The wrath of the storms fury reigns
Runs frantically through these halls
Searching for shelter among empty walls
The storm continues to develop
I let the wind, my heart envelope
Then, Succumbs my soul to this night
These feelings, I no longer fight
Allow them now to freely flow
And so the rest of my life shall go
No longer the trial concealing
But allowing the free flow of each feeling
Each emotion I shall not spurn
Til He says it's now my turn
There will joy everlasting be
No longer mourning for my loves or me

Pray for Me, My Saints (12/18/18)

They say to just breathe
As if you'll release from me
Like it's a magic trick
Do it and your memory won't stick
I won't be affected anymore
My sadness will go out the door
But it doesn't work that way
I've tried to exhale, but every day
The clouds remain over my head
You're still here, though you're dead
Try to get my mind off you
Doesn't work, no matter what I do
Saying "I'm through" and trying
To wash away mem'ries of you dying
Made the thoughts come back stronger
I realize you'll be around much longer
Putting you out of view on a shelf
Isn't even that much help
'Cause you just come back down
And circle back around
Snuff you out like a candle
You come back stronger than I can handle
Close you like a good book
But I return because I'm hooked
So remind me of your Heavenly gains
And pray for me, my little saints

A New Kind of Gone (12/31/18)

When we leave our saints who we buried behind, and we have to continue without them here, and then we leave behind their own birth year...it's a new kind of gone

It's been a year
Since you left
Now that year's gone
Of it, too, I'm bereft

It was the year
I had you around
Now you're not here
It's no more to be found

Left it all behind
Resides in the past
I turn around and find
Nothing earthly lasts

Why do I keep yearning
To find you in this grief
The world keeps turning
Each moment here is brief

When instead I should
Be looking to the future and smile
Knowing that I could
Be with you eternally after a while

Please, Lord, let my body align
With whatever Your will
And so, too, my feeble mind
That with You, I might be still

And not dwell on this new kind of gone
Along with the last time they were here
Help me to move along
With grace in the coming years

This Place (6/10/19)

My last hCG blood draw is June 15th. I'm feeling bittersweet...

How will I feel
When the last needle is removed?
Soon I shall see
The days creep up behind
Like a stranger lurking in the dark
As if I've never met grief before
It's a new thief every time
This one doth not beg to differ
It lies in wait for me, unlike
The others, which took me by surprise
I feel this one breathing down my neck
I can't shake it away
I know I must turn around and greet it
Facing it head on
Even here, my heart refuses to
Acknowledge the task lying ahead
It seeks refuge this time in words
Thinking it only needs to write down the
Lonely pain that is to come
The future is already numb
To me
I will do as before
On the selected day, I will, like a robot,
Get in my van and drive the
Seven minutes to the familiar place
Sit as before after turning off the van
Take my purse and open the door
Close it behind me and lock
The door
All meticulously done. Each time,
The place feels like home.
Perhaps it's because I'm reminded of
You and maybe you're there? Both of you?
I approach the door to the place and pull it
Open unphased, reminded again of the

Reasons why I'm brought here
Sign in, sit and wait. They call me to the window again, to confirm details
Then back to the chair
The one that's not a recliner,
No, it doesn't offer comfort in that way
But it is where the needle meets me
As if to withdraw one more piece of life
And so I'm reminded of her presence
However brief

I watch as the elixir is drawn away
From my arm, one more piece of her
It seems, though each time now
The numbers say she's gone completely
And it remains incomprehensible to me
Why this place is where I want to be
Why the last time shall be bittersweet
The last time I'll be reminded of she
Who graced my womb for 8 short weeks
It will happen one more time this Saturday
And then it will stop, suddenly the spot light
Is turned away to another
Someone who has gone through it all
These times are just leftovers though
I get no attention
I'm but a number and a name
They just take what they want and
Follow protocol
But then that's all
No more calls
I'm expected to live life as it should be lived
When someone hasn't loved and lost
Wondering when and if
There'll be a next time
And if that next time happens, will there be
A repeat loss?
No, that is overlooked. They only want
Numbers.

But they have other patients
So til we meet again,
I once more fall by the wayside
After this last time
At this place I knew so well
Had become so familiar with
After this time, I'll be in the clear
Based on the protocol.
Oh how I wish to educate
Everyone on how there's more
Than protocol, needles, and this place
Look beyond that all to the memories
The pain we've faced.
All contained and symbolized by
This place
So I soon shall leave it behind
No longer there to remind
Me of that mid-August day
Praying I have no need to meet here again
But wishing I didn't have to leave so soon
This is the last draw.
The last little bit of the physical memory of she who left so soon
The sorrow might my heart consume
Grief might go on and return
As I'm reminded of what I'm to leave behind
Yet that which I must both keep and leave behind
Sorrows and love that's mine and in my mind
Been skating through knowing this day
would arrive. I'm left to wonder and ponder on how, after this day passes,
Oh, what will my heart now beat for?
Will it again feel the heavy emptiness
The weight of my losses it presumably had
Progressed towards the healing that comes
On this earth?
Will I once more spiral into the night tunnel
Of depression?
What things will happen after the needle
Once more is placed and removed

The last drops of the reminder of your life
Withdrawn and analyzed
I hesitantly climb off my pedestal where
Time and time again you were crowned
Yours and your brothers names always
Thrown around
All gone are the reminders given me all times
I have gone through the motions
In this place

Letting Go (8/29/19)

Mama wakes in the night
Seems to be no reason or rhyme
Something's not quite right
And it won't turn out okay this time

She knew chances were slim
Yet still gave everything to this babe
Two weeks later she sees him
And she holds his tiny frame

It was all she had to hold on to
Since it was his time to let go
She didn't don't know what else to do
As she struggled through her lowest low
She knows some things we hold on to
Even when they're letting go

In the life that followed
She walked through it in a daze
Her thoughts were shallow
But she held on to hope through this phase

It was all she had to hold on to
After her baby had to go
She just kept plowing through
As she worked through her lowest low
She knew what she had to do
While she was there letting go

This is her new normal now
She knows there's no turning back
Yet she can't help but question how
She's supposed to go on with what she lacks

Hard when nothing's there to hold on to
When there's no real letting go
Of the memory of all she went through
When God called her baby to go
Love and memories are what she holds onto
While the rest is letting go

She knows from what she's been through
Sometimes love means letting go

Grasping for God

Looking to the Future

Carrying On (9/29/18)

I write here about my lost love for a passion that seemed I'd never lose, a work I desired so much to become involved in. The world of a doula. Once I had my second miscarriage, I seemed to lose my passion, triggered by that very thing which used to bring me such innocent joy.

Where do I go from here?
How do I return to there?
How do I erase the fear?
How do I escape this snare?

I used to thrive innocently on
The bliss of pregnancy and birth
But that passion seems gone
From my babies' loss left this joys dearth

No longer do I care as much
To hear of love's labor
The mother and baby's first touch
Has my delight fallen out of favor?

Where do I go from this place?
What's to help me on my journey healing
When can I at birth show my face?
How do I triumph o'er this feeling?

Return to the exuberance I once knew
Maturing from my sorrow of this time
Seeing her labor and birth full through
Remembering my losses are not her crime

To doula with all my heart
Not integrate emotions of my trauma
I need to do my part
To support the radiant mama

Prayer to my saints (10/2/18)

May the earthly loss of you two
Yield heavenly healing of my bruise
May you ask for healing of my heart
And help me continue to do my part

Pray he leads me in what to do
And if I'm meant to Doula, carry me through
May you and all saints and angels
Flank me on all sides and guard each angle

May he bring me joy and peace
In witnessing what my passion used to be
May he help me stay always strong
And bring my saints Marky and Lucy along

May from the pain of your deaths mem'ry
He remind me of his eternal Glory
From this lonely, painful sorrow set me free
May the joy of Heaven ne'er let go of me

Moving Within (11/18/18)

Faking til I make it still wasn't working for me. So friends told me to see a therapist and after my first session, I realized it was God giving me another chance, a chance to come alive again, but living a different life. A new normal. And that change began moving me within.

I'm not yet done
She said to the Son
Of course He understands
It's because of the fall of man
So He let her live
She had more to give
Needed time to come
From her dark to her new home
A brand new life she'd lead
Living by a different creed
Once she took that fall
Naught was the same at all
So to live she would begin
To find a new normal within

See You Again (1/1/19)

It's been a year
I brush past the tear
Wave off the fear
It's a new dawn

It's makin' me strong
Dancin' to a new song
Moving right along
Never forgetting you're gone

Doesn't matter much now
Nothing I can do about
All that matters is how
I live to see you again

Live life so well
Within me God dwells
Keep me from Hell
Guide me to Heaven

Follow the straight and narrow line
Evil Temptations decline
To His Will resign
My path to peace within

Do this and hold you inside
Take your memory for a ride
Your intercessions my guide
'Til I see you again

Life (1/25/19)

I took the time off for a few weeks surrounding the first anniversary of Marky's death, delivery, and burial. It was good to allow myself that time to reflect on that part of my life. I carry him with me always, but my job with Marky is done, he is in Heaven, my goal achieved. Now I must focus on helping my other littles, asking his intercession and help praying for God's grace and strength to bring my other kiddos and my husband to Heaven. The goal of life here on earth isn't just to live for this life in the present, but to live so we can have life eternal after these trials on earth are finished. May we take all we have been given and multiply the talents, so in the end, by God's mercy and grace, be welcomed into Heaven. May we live this life according to the master's Will so that in the end He might say: well done, my good and faithful servant.

Open my eyes and
Lie there in bed
Still can't move forward
Despite all I've said

Still trying my best
To live this life well
With these struggles every day
I really can't tell

Am I doing His Will
Each moment is spinning
As I act and feel
I don't know who's winning

So much confusion
And the desire's still there
Being pulled in all directions
The world doesn't care

Trying hard to
Move through each day
This time for me is still
Needed and that's okay

It's more important to
Allow my heart and body to feel
So I don't feel guilty for
Doin' what I need to heal

Every day balancing
What with my life here needs done?
And taking time putting pieces together
According to the Spirit of the Father and Son

As I move through these times
Slowly adjusting to life again
He puts all the pieces in place
To help me with this new life begin

A Doula's Call (1/30/19)

I firmly believe I've had the various pregnancy and birth experiences so that God-willing, I'll be able to better support women in the future, women who go through all kinds of battles. To show them they CAN come up on the other side and to always have hope. This is no different.

Even through the pain
The love will remain
That which I desired before
The passion that ran through my core
The thing loss had suppressed
My fears I have confessed
I know this grief ain't a sin
It's ok to stay within
To guard myself a while
To gradually become my smile
To know this journey breaking me apart
Will eventually lead me back to my heart
The thing for which I used to long
For which I had a love so strong
Will once again appear
And once more become so dear
And all the things I used to know
Will once again within me grow
It will all happen in God's perfect time
Not on the change of my dime
And like a flower that matures from a bud
I'll follow what God sent coursing through my blood
For would the passion of His mother be erased
When the trial of His death she courageously faced
She dealt with such pain and grief
But never let her sorrow be joys thief

She's the doula to who's role I aspire
I trust she'll set my heart once more afire
To support those through day and night
Whether things go wrong or right
To be there through their labor's pain
My help shall never wane
To love despite my fall
To answer this, a doula's call

Learnin' to Live Again (6/12/19)

Got to the hospital that morn at seven
By then you'd made it to heaven
There was nothin we could have done
A saintly daughter joined our saintly son
Moved through life in the months to follow
Every part within me felt hollow
Put one foot in front of the other and then
I started learnin' to live again

Learnin' to live again
Learnin' to live with back when
And all the while
Forcin' myself to smile
Open new chapter in my soul
Something that'll make me whole
A new me cuz the old one's wearin' thin
So I'm learnin' to live again

Sit staring out the window sill
Nothin but a load of time to kill
But my tears rolled out with the tide
I felt a new kinda whole inside
Things had to change
I couldn't stay the same
Couldn't go back to where I've been
Gotta move forward, learnin' to live again

Learnin' to live again
Learnin' to live with back when
And all the while
Forcin' my smile
A new chapter in my soul
There to make me whole
A new me cuz the old one's wearin' thin
Makin' me learn to live again

When my sands of time are runnin' low
And it's almost time for me to go
Am I gonna regret the life I coulda lived?
Gonna miss what ya had left to give?
Give that gift before the light grows dim
No time like the present to learn to live again

Start livin' again
Despite what happened back when
And all the while
Share my smile
A new chapter in my soul
There to make me whole
A new me cuz the old one's wearin' thin
Makin' me learn to live again

Finding Faith

No More Doubts (Jan 17, 2018)
(Written for Mark William, miscarried at 16weeks)

So often I have sunk into the thought process of wishing Mark was still here, but he's gone. This is all well, but it helps me to remember that earth is not to be our final resting place, that our beautiful saints, though missed sorely, are in their final resting Place. Safe with Our Father, Who art in Heaven

So many what ifs cross my mind
But each answer proves me oh so blind
For each question seems a doubt
That since he's gone, he's missing out
How dare I question why
When I know he's with a great Guy
Why do I question what he is getting after birth
And compare to what he'd receive on earth

For love, he has his Family in Heaven
With the Spirit, he's an advocate for our family of seven
For guidance, he has His Father's Hand
For food, he has the Son of Man

I weep because he has no more time here
But really, what need I fear?
No time to deal with the worldly way
Gone straight to Heaven, never led astray

I shed tears because I loved
But rejoice, for he's with Love above
I cry for the loss of his little soul
But rejoice upon reaching my goal

As parents we all yearn
We seek and our hearts burn
Though the chances seem oh, so faint
For our littles to all become a saint

Why then should we mourn
When they end this earthly sojourn
When they leave this life seemingly quaint
To join in heavenly joys as a saint?

One Month a Saint (2/17/18)

Anniversaries will always be a moment in time that brings you back, no matter how well you are doing leading up to then. I learned not to be surprised if, around that time, my arms and legs returned to feeling like lead, if my babies were the only thoughts in my head. Don't see it as a bad thing. This is how it will go; this is how your new normal is formed. Be not afraid, Our Lord goes before you always. Follow Him, keep your eyes on Him, and He will give you rest. Remember, He suffered, too, and took on all the suffering of the world during His Passion and Crucifixion.

One month ago
God brought you to His Joyful Abode
In doing so
He changed my earthly load

In my heart and mind
I carry this tiny cross
Uniting it to Christ's
Whene'er I feel my loss

Heaven gained a lil saint
This is true
God knew I needed one
And He hath chosen you

From heaven,
You bring me peace and joy
God knew what He was doing
When He gave me you, baby boy

I needed more God in my life
Without Him, it's dark
And so, He helped me
By leaving His Mark

God (8/6/18)

Those times I lose focus, and for those times I turn inward to see my suffering, those times and always are the times He is with me. That is Love as it should be, the love I should emulate, always thinking of the other, as He did on the road to Calvary and on the Cross, despite pain and suffering.

Fall asleep and the day is gone
Wake up to a new one, there is dawn
That's the way the world may go
He remains the same although
Ages continue to pass
Nothing here shall last
He always has my heart
As He did from the start
This love unending is
This love remains always His

Resurfacing (10/28/18)

So often when grieving, I feel as if this is all life is meant to be, that is, a constant feeling of drowning. No relief. That this is how it SHOULD be. So often, I'm reminded that I was not created for this and through prayer and God's Mercy, He keeps me afloat through it all. He helps me resurface to where He wants me to be.

In the throes of grief
Stuck here for a while
It's just like a thief
Stealing away my smile

Feeling stuck inside
A ship that's going down
In my own Titanic I abide
Trying not to drown

Frozen mostly in the water
I scream, but feel my voice freeze
I think I'm getting hotter
But the waves of grief just tease

I just hold onto this wood
Get used to this cold
Behaving as I should
As if I'll be here til I'm old

Through my dimmed, deceived lens
A beguiling light appears
For a moment, I don't wonder when
I'll overcome my fears

And I feel at the end of my rope
Like I can't take much more
But I remember it's God giving me hope
Showing me what's in store

Though my faith is shaken
I'll eventually make the leap
Yes my heart is breakin'
He'll rescue me from these waters deep

He knows well this sorrow
This tiny cross I carry
With Him, there's hope in tomorrow
Sit with my heart so weary

He's with me all this time
Walking this road with me
I know alone I'm blind
But with His grace I can see
He'll bring me to the surface
To that light from my dream
The cold waters that used to encompass
No longer daunting as they seemed

My Captain always at the wheel
Saves me from icebergs in my way
With His grace in The Eucharistic Meal
Carries me to safety on my final day

My Constant (11/4/18)

Through life's ups and downs, our Lord always remains there for us, always unchanging, our Constant.

For richer or poorer
Til death do us part
Love every day with
Each beat of my heart

The ups and the downs
Come every hour
May He hold us together
When this life turns sour

So many things
Interrupt this flow
And til the end
That's how it'll go

Love and loss
All part of life
But with Him at the helm
We'll remain man and wife

When all hope seems gone
And I turn to you
With His grace overflowing
We're bound to make it through

Seasons start to change
Like in Fall when
Shortly after, begins winter
And the cold is ushered in

After a blissful spring
And summer of healing
This change in season
Has sent me reeling

I struggle with hopelessness
And I finally start to see
In my deepest abyss
He remains in me

Thoughts permeate my heart
With His peaceful light
He is our Constant
In the darkest hour of our night

Prayer Uplifted (11/16/18)

Many times, my days have been difficult to move through. I do it because I have others who rely on me. I know I cannot do this on my own, and so I am learning to take this heavy cross and rather than focus on the pain, turn it into a prayer uplifted.

Arise from this bed
He said to the dead
Who took up his mat?
And did just that
So we, too, shall rise
Wipe the dark from our eyes
His Love washes away tears
We've shed all these years
Our burdens gone
At the new age's dawn
We are no longer alone
As we kneel before His Throne
Our struggle meets its end
It no longer has bearing when
We remember His cross
He's carried our loss
As we wander this life
Hearts pierced by a knife
Heaviness of our hardships
Satan, at our heals, nips
And try as we might
Pray for others as we fight
With all the prayer we can muster
This life less lackluster
Help me, Oh Lord
I struggle with every word
Help me through this life you've gifted
Turn my struggle into a prayer uplifted

Mary's Statue (11/29/18)

Gazing upon a statue of Our Lady, Christ's Mother, a peace overcame me…

Days flying fast
Heart comes to a halt
I'm not moving past
I'm the one at fault

Wrapped up in my game,
It's hard to see me through
I invoke your name
And I look at you

I feel myself let go
I know it'll be alright
You told me so
Shining your Son's Light

I am so tense
Upon sight of you, release
When once I rode the fence
Now in my sight, His peace

Crush the serpent of pain
Crush the serpent of sorrow
My struggles are not in vain
They have meaning for my tomorrow

Return to my day
Feel again the sting
But I now know the way
That peace at once shall bring

I need only return my gaze
To see your cloak and face
Wipe away my hearts haze
Bring me to your place

That sacred spot in my yard
Where your statue stands
The evil of pain you discard
Upon the folding of your hands

For your prayer, so pure,
Is always perfectly aimed
Your words bring my cure
From my heart, so terribly pained

From a sorrow you know
A life you understand so well
You saw your own Son's life go
So we could be saved from Hell

So, to my struggles, I return
Thinking of His sacrifice
That I may live so not to burn
And in the end be pleasing to His eyes

Brighten my hearts agony
Oh, Mary, standing there
May you always remind me
Turn my heart to Him, not despair

The Star (12/16/18)

The journey isn't an easy one, we won't follow an easy path, but it will be worth it in the end to remain on the straight and narrow and follow the Star.

The God-Man knows our sufferings
On Christmas His gentle peace brings
He knows our every struggle, pain, and thought
For with His life, our freedom bought

He came to Earth a babe so poor
And left the same, op'ning Heaven's door
For the richness we all yearn to buy
Isn't to be found in this life

We seek it and want to avoid the pain
Forgetting it's the path to heavenly gain
We walk with forced gait
While, for our future, hurriedly wait

So on this solemn night of nights
When he came to set things right
Stop where I am and see
This life's path isn't all about me

May this strenuous journey shape my heart
May it form my life falling apart
Building it into something new
A sparkle in the morning dew

To seek the greater good it doth teach
That for something higher I might reach
Like the wise men traveled from afar
Lead my heart to the Heavenly Star

Mary's Way (12/23/18)

It's an even harder road to travel when you and your husband are on different paths of grief. Through the difficult times, may I meditate on yours, Our Mother, for you handled them with such grace.

You were chosen and said yes
Then gave birth to the One
Gone then was your Joseph
For the death of your only Son

Contemplating your sorrow
Knowing you'd lose your Boy
New beginning tomorrow
My hope is in your joy

As I seek to resurface
From things which bring me down
Praying for help fulfilling my purpose
And turn my life around

Days I've lost to pride
Those I can't recover now
Can only live my vocation in life
Honoring my covenant and vows

So I move forward today
Though we are so far apart
Pondering, Our Lady's Way,
Keeping all things in my heart

Christmas Light (12/24/18)

I tried to fill the hole within me by comfort eating. I gained weight and felt worse, nothing was healed. And so I pray instead for the Joy of Christmas to fill me, not to pass me by. I'm too weak to do it myself, but humble myself for You to imbue me with Christmas Light.

My heart continues to sink
The hole continues to grow
As the world is on the brink
Of forgetting all woe

Tryin' to see instead
The reason for the joy
In a makeshift bed
The newborn Infant Boy

I sit alone on this silent night
Staring at the sky
Praying the Christmas Light
Doesn't pass me by

I hear a child's laugh
The happiness on their faces
I realize in the past
I've sought joy in the wrong places

As if comforts of the world
Would make things all right
As each moment unfurled
I realize joy comes from Christmas's Light

I sit here on this silent night
Staring at the sky
Watching for the Christmas Light
Knowing He's my sorrow's why

He's all of life's reason
For Whom we all live
And this is the season
We celebrate all He had to give

So I sit with Him on this silent night
Staring at the sky
Allowing the Peace of the Christmas Light
To come dwell inside

This Joy (12/25/18)

One more, I ponder the difficulty of dealing with the difference of how some men and women deal with grief. Some women are relational (like I am) and some men prefer to take it out on doing useful things. I know there are other ways people cope, Know that your friends or relatives might be trying to help, but in their own language. They might be grieving, too, and it might come out differently than it does for you. I know the languages of expressing it differ. I know I must ultimately rely on Christ and trust in Him for my strength, but struggle in knowing what that looks like.

This joy I'd like to feel
Is held up deep within
Like a box with a seal
Waiting to be opened again

I hear everyone enjoy
That which comes with this day
Playing with each new toy
But I don't know what to say

I try to join in the laughter
But it's short lived and
I know from hereafter
I need less consolation from man

To seek not where I thought I belonged
For, Love from my Lord and King
Ultimate happiness and joy prolonged
Is better than any worldly thing

So to Him my heart should turn
I'll have no more regrets
And I shall earthly solace spurn
And from Heav'n, true Joy begets

Prayer for My Day (12/27/18)

Lord, guide me this and every day
Mother Mary, help me follow His Way
That everything I say and do
Imitates Him and you
May I accept God's Grace and love
To grow closer to Him Above
To see my losses as gain
That my love for Him shall not wane
That instead my struggles bring me close
Answer my saints plea that my love grows
To see through today's pain and sorrow
The joys of each day and it's tomorrow
I ask for strength as mom and wife
To live out my vocation in this life
So when with this exile, my heart is done
I may be with You and them in the next one

My Little Way (1/1/19)

Through my losses I am reminded how I need to do everything, big or small, with love. It is following this way that will bring me closer to Him, which is my ultimate desire.

Still hard to breathe
I don't know why
Try to forget
Comes back to mind
Take a deep breath
My thoughts rewind
Your name races through my head
I try to be fine

A smile crosses my face
All's well for a moment
After the fleeting peace
I return to the torment
This is my cross
Why do I scorn it
I should embrace it
My heart's love's dormant

So, I return to life
And live for each day
Allowing each memory
To come and pass as it may
No longer pawn it off
As if I'm trying to betray
The sacrifice I'm called to offer
In my own little way

In Adoration (1/16/19)

I took my husband's Adoration hour this morning in the chapel and aim to do so more often. It was a peaceful hour. In the midst of the silence, I heard from Him and I responded in my silence.

Him: Come to this Place
And dwell in My Presence
You bear your face
Dear earthly peasant
You try so hard
To make heard your prayer
I continue to remove each chard
Remaining in your heart there

Me: Lord, it's been a year
I lose more of the heavy sadness
Each time You come near
And instill Your Joy and Gladness
The question then is no longer why
I carry this, my cross
But rather how can I
Honor this, my once perceived loss?

Him: Silence once more
My servant who seeks Me
Allow Me to open a new door
And lead you to see
So much I have planned for you
Just trust Me to lead
And in everything that you do
You'll be planting My Love's seed

Me: You Lord, You I trust
And let You take my hand
Remembering I was created from dust
And shall return to it again
That in all Your Mighty Power
You share a mother's grief
And every single hour
You hold our lives so brief

Give it to God (1/17/19)

So it hit a little bit ago. My arms are feeling empty and heavy. Feeling partly numb and knowing it was in this and all moments I'm called to give it to God. So I did. And though I feel the heaviness all around, I'm feeling it with a smile. Around my other kids who still need me to mom. I pause to recall, feel it through, and move forward as He wants me to.

The light was here
Dark attempted to push it aside
So now I'm feeling alone
Only God knows what's inside
With intent and focus
I moved through the day
I thought the sadness had
Mostly faded away
But as I sit here and think
After the day is gone
Wondering if my feelings suppressed
Were also feeling alone
As each hour unfurled
I tried to live it well
Thought I was better
But knew only time would tell
So now the time arrives
Near this day's end
When I think of my empty arms
And can no longer pretend
With His Grace I still have hope
While with heaviness I trod
Taking my sorrows and suffering
And continue giving them to God

God's Call (1/30/19)

Ever since losing Lucy, I've felt numb towards the doula world and felt bad for feeling that way, especially since I had taken the training and fulfilled that part of my passion. But when I keep wishing it to just return to me, I find I'm wasting the time I have now with MY family...those who come second only to God.

My heart needs to restart
Let healing do its part
First break me down
Then I'll circle 'round
Shedding the skin of who I used to be
Showing fully the newly transformed me
The product of the lines on my face
Of the trials in my short life have faced
I can't jump to that person yet
Need to release things briefly and not fret
And maybe I'll return to them down the road
Enjoy right now the blessings bestowed
Not waste a single moment is this
Replacing reality with my future wish
But let go of that hold
Focus on the present gold
Love those who I treasure
Think not of it as lost time measured
To value all I've been given now
And not question when or how
For every moment filled with want
Is giving in to the devil's taunt
Once more avoid the fall
By instead, answering God's Call

Keepin the Faith (2/9/19)

It's so hard to be fervent right now, to do much more than to show up at Mass and stare at the Tabernacle, wherein resides the Hidden Jesus. And maybe to ask Him for the strength and courage to keep facing each day...and for Him to help me to keep on keepin the Faith.

In the midst of this sorrow
I wonder where You are
How will You help each tomorrow
When it seems You're so far
I feel alone in this room
Even as I pray
In this darkness and gloom
Why would You stay?
It's such a painful place
And I struggle staying here
But if not for Your Face
How much more would I fear?

Not knowing what tomorrow brings
And not wanting to find out
Because my heart no longer sings
Instead it is shrouded in doubt
All because of this test
You've allowed happen to me
It proves I can't be at my best
When I don't turn to Thee

Lord, to whom would I go?
You are eternal life
No one else I know
Gives me strength during strife
When I'm at my lowest low
And wearily I turn
Your mercy You show
Your love You shall not spurn

Lord it's so hard each time
To stop seeking earthly joy
When it's so convincingly sublime
To not recognize the devil's ploy
To see this as a call from Heaven
To listen daily to what You saith
For me to go where You're Hidden
And to keep on keepin' the Faith

His Pull (2/23/19)

As I stood there in the shower, I noted how difficult it's been to breathe since losing them, this heavy emptiness in me takes on another form. The pain of loss drags down my breaths and makes it hard to inhale or exhale fully.

Closer to my saints
With this broken heart in my chest
They bring me closer to You
Down the path You know best
This pit in my stomach rises
With my chest when I breathe
Holding hostage the emotion tied
To losing them inside of me
Thinking with each breath so
Intensely of what I know
Can't release this emptiness
For it's too heavy to let go
So down my Calvary
With the weight of my sins inside
Akin to this empty feeling left
By they who no longer reside
How hard it is now
How much harder it would be
If I didn't carry this my cross
During this life's purgatory
The meaning of all this, I
Won't know as of yet
I know not Your mind
But this is my best bet
To take it as it is
And suffer the pain in full
No longer pushing with my might
When You give me a pull

Your Words (2/23/19)

I hear something
In my mind
But I return to
What I left behind
I beg for your answer
But stay in a bind
Yet I still hold on
To my earthly finds

Why'd God create me
as a social creature?
I talk and need to hear His words
I'm a beseecher

I know we have the Bible
I want Him to speak to me
I know He suffered alone on the Cross,
but I'm not as strong as He

The spirit is willing
but the flesh is weak,
this deaf doubting Thomas
needs to HEAR Him speak

I ask You please
But I don't know what for
Fall to my knees
Yet You give me more

I don't even have the strength
To ask in prayer
For You to give me strength
To avoid the devil's lair

Why'd You give me passion for doula'ing
Only to suffer remorse
To lose that passion after I lost Lucy
Once I'd already taken the course

I know all things are for me to learn
To understand sacrifice
I know Your will be done
But knowing Your will would be nice

What would You have me do
What's Your plan for my life
To set me on a sure path
Then to cut like a knife

Here I stand on this breached road
So now I am stuck and stopped
Trying to understand the meaning
Of life's picture cut and cropped

Where would You have me go
Where the paths now diverge
If I follow one,
Will they once again merge

How do I listen to You
When all I get are choices
And when I ask Your guidance
I hear not Your voice

But remain in this mire
Just continue to be stuck
When I ask for help,
Your answer is clear as mud

Lord I know you've given us
The Bible and your commands
But my feeble mind doesn't follow
Neon signs are all it understands

So, grant me through your Spirit
A growth of His Gifts
I can't understand as You wish me to
Lest wisdom and understanding be swift

Counsel me first in fear of Him
And grant me fortitude to be still
Piety that I might grow closer and so
Then knowledge of His Will

Help me to use all trials and successes
On this path to holiness I trod
In the way I glorify Him with the good
In the rough might I also glorify God

No Rest (3/11/19)

Weary and broken
No respite in
The words that're spoken
To you

The world continues
Spinning around
You travel each avenue
You've found

You continue in
This lonely path
While others have gone
Away

It's not their pain
Not suff'ring to bear
So you meet your rain
Alone

There is no rest
On this earth
Your heart put to the test
Of love

You realize as before
Our hearts remain restless
'Til they rest once more
In Him

The Joy in Me (3/24/19)

True joy isn't necessarily found in what I seek and what I think holds joy. True joy is in being open to His Will and inviting Him in to carry you through every instance of your life.

The joy in me
Ain't what I thought it to be
It doesn't surround
Me here on this ground
Can't find it searching within
Can't see it til I'm lookin' at Him

Hey you with the face
Stay in this place
Don't run, don't hide
This is where you abide
I know they all say
You'll be okay
They don't wanna hear more
Hard to explore
But that pain you feel
Is no less real
So spend time where you are
The Light ain't that far
He's with you, you know
He'll stay wherever you go
Your emotions, don't bury
I know it's kinda scary
You must travel this road
No matter how heavy your load
Cry all the tears
Release all your fears
Lest your heart runs amuck
When your feelings get stuck
Don't keep anything inside
This ain't no place to hide
Gotta travel the whole way through
That part ain't up to you

Can't hold it in forever
Not if ya wanna get better
Gotta take it step by step
Though there's no way to prep
Just keep takin it as it comes
Don't start the next part til this is done

The joy in me
Ain't what I thought it to be
It doesn't surround
Me here on this ground
Can't find it searching within
Can't see it til I'm lookin' at Him

For the longest time
I was sublime
But once I was in a bind
And lost my peace of mind
My earth was shaken
I was mistaken
My heart was breakin'
All along I was fakin'
I lost what was inside
Life rolled out with the tide
Had to confront my grief
I thought it was Joy's thief
But it returned, to my relief
When I turned a new leaf
Thought sorrow didn't belong
But I was wrong
With God, I became strong
Sang a new song
In darkness I grope
At the end of my rope
All I did was mope
But then I found hope
Spirit is willin' but the flesh is weak
Lots of me needs to be tweaked
Future often looks bleak

Thought I could get by without a squeak
I was put in my place
Pain left without a trace
After seein' God's face
Saved by His grace
I took the fall
Wasn't gettin by at all
God dropped the ball
And I answered His call
I had no other choice
I had no other voice
Quiet the unnecessary noise
In the end I rejoice
I thought I was through
Nothin left to do
Didn't know what I was gettin into
But I Finally turned to You

Afraid of what I'd see
Didn't think I'd like this me
Wasn't sure who I was gonna be
Wanted a list A to Z
I was a doubting Thomas
But You took me as I was
Forgave me and loved me
It's what Your Mercy does

The joy in me
Ain't what I thought it to be
It doesn't surround
Me here on this ground
Can't find it searching within
Can't see it 'til I'm lookin' at Him

Loving You (5/29/19)

Why do I worry about earthly things
When I know time here on earth is but a fling
Why put so much weight on my pain
It's a stepping stone to heav'nly gain
I'll receive but naught
If I continue giving much thought
So turn my heart and give all to you
For You surely know what to do
I give all this useless stuff
To You cuz I've had enough
You'll make all things new and good
Because I never could
Move past What I cannot do
And think only of loving you

The Lighted Way (7/13/19)

The spirit is willing but the flesh is weak
Heart beats too loud to hear You speak
Your words come in, but my soul does seek
To change around, Your thoughts to tweak
Hearing You my future seems bleak

You feel so far away
Healing words You come to say
My body keeps you at bay
It all seems impossible today
To follow Your Lighted Way

So I'm here stuck in my mind
Dismiss You and I fall blind
Yet Your Mercy remains so kind
I keep seeking, trying to find
Earthly relief and You remind

Me You aren't that far away
Healing words You come to say
My body keeps you at bay
It's not impossible today
To follow Your Lighted Way

Now I call my body to retreat
So Your healing here should meet
Once more evil finds defeat
Death has no sting, His life's more sweet
In days of despair, I put this on repeat

You aren't that far away
Your healing words came to stay
When my body keeps you at bay
You make it possible each day
To follow Your Lighted Way

Sidelines (7/17/19)

Those times we fight what God is trying to give us. It's much easier if we just sit on the sidelines and let Him work!

Watching my life ride by
From behind the painted lines
Made by tears on my face
Over things I can't replace
I repeatedly fall down
You pick me up from the ground

I push and You pull
Then You make my life full
I admit my defeat
Then you make me complete
You air out my sad
And replace it with glad
Turn bad to good times
When all I can do is sit on the sidelines

Fallen numerous times
Guilty of the same ol' crimes
You pull me upright
Never uptight
Always ready to forgive
When I forget how to live

I give a push, then You pull
You make my life full
I take a back seat
While you make me complete
You air out the sad
And replace it with glad
Turn bad to good times
When all I can do is sit on the sidelines

In moments I don't know what to do
You're there to drag me through

I give a push, then You pull
You make my life full
I take a back seat
While you make me complete
You air out the sad
And replace it with glad
Turn bad to good times
When all I can do is sit on the sidelines

God Made Me You (7/26/19)

I had four
I was ready for more
So God made me you
Kept you inside
For a short little while
'Cause God made me you

For a moment in time
Your heart beat with mine
I knew when you were through
'Cause God made me you

In the blink of an eye
You went to the sky
After God made me you
You weren't meant to stay
I know that today
Since God made me you

I cherish that moment in time
Your heart beat with mine
Loved you through and through
'Cause God made me you

I can ask every why
Won't know til I die
And that'll be alright
I'll just trust your silent goodbye
'Cause God made me you

It was a brief moment in time
When your heart beat with mine
Now is your turn to guide me through
'Cause God made me you

Prayer for Peace In Grief (7/27/19)

I wrote this when I was struggling seeing friends and family pregnant while I struggled seeing my body struggle to return to some semblance of normalcy, even almost a year after my second miscarriage, wishing so much for another life on this earth, but knowing not my will, but Yours, always be done.

God take this jealousy away from me
Help unite my suffering closer to Thee
Let not my heart
Be torn apart
Or turned to stone
When I feel alone
Help me in times like these
Turn to You on my knees
Handing over all my thoughts
Help me do as I ought
And realize even though they're gone
Life will continue to move along
Give me strength to ride this ship
With Your Courage, please equip
My fallen, prideful humanity
To, with burdened eyes always be
Your handmaid on this tear-filled earth
Even amidst death before birth
I have not the strength myself to rise
Be Ye my strong surprise
To help me think of others first
Though in this desert my soul does thirst
For new life to come to me again
Where six had previously been

Four I was privileged to keep with me here
Two I was blessed to have forever near
Who bring a daily dose of Paradise
Dawn to dusk and another sunrise
May the physical pain Your Pardon be
Coursing through the veins inside of me
Take this opportunity disguised as less
See it as one more way my life, You bless
May You with Your Mighty Power employ
And lead me always to Your fount of Joy
May Your Mercy show me my earthly loss
Bring me closer to You through your Cross
And though the wood be heavy still
Make me the handmaid of Your Will
And let this pain and sorrow once more
Give way to Joy

Holding Back (8/8/19)

In my darkest moments following my miscarriages, when I think
of the unthinkable, it's God Who pulls
me through.

Goin head to head every day
Battling words I can't bear to say
Feeling the pull towards the worst
But just as I'm about to burst
I feel the Lord coming near
Suddenly stops every fear

Moving forward without holding back
As He helps me pick up my slack
Conquering the demons that befall me
Reject their bids when they call me
Put up Gods shield when they attack
He moves me forward without holding back

As the clouds cover my life
And the hurt falls from my eyes
He takes away my pride and
Once more I try to begin again

Moving forward without holding back
He's there to pick up my slack
Conquering the demons that befall me
Reject their bids when they call me
Put up Gods shield when they attack
He moves me forward without holding back

He asks me to give Him my heart
Promises to heal me when it falls apart

He keeps me Moving forward without holding back
Always right there to pick up my slack
Conquering the demons that befall me
Reject their bids when they call me
Put up His shield when they attack
He moves me forward without holding back

Everything to Lose (8/14/19)

Here I am alone in this place
Once more
Nothin' to show but lines on my face
But what for
Walking around aimlessly
Trying to find a place for me

I search in the dark
For some kinda spark
Even if I put up a fight
I can't make my own Light
Realize I've got nothin' to prove
And everything to lose

Pinch me and I'll wake up
Pour life's elixir in my mourning cup
Take away this terrible dream
Things can't be as bad as they seem
I wished for two lines
They were given, taken, never mine

I search in the dark
For some kinda spark
Even if I put up a fight
I can't make my own Light
Realize I've got nothin' to prove
And everything to lose

This is my cross
Here is my crown
With God here to lift me
When I am down
Up to me to let Him in
Up to me when to begin

In the midst of my dark
He is my spark
Shows mercy when I fight
He is my own Light
I don't need to prove
'Cause He won't let me lose

Flowers on the Vine (10/4/19)

Up from the dirt
Where you were laid to rest
Sprouts something new
That withstands the test
And so buds

Flowers on the vine
That cover up the hardships
Beat into this heart of mine
Like a pretty piece of paper
With a flat line
Masking the painful thorns
Like flowers on a vine

The rain falls down
To make 'em grow
And from the cold drops on the ground
New beauty flows

Those flowers on the vine
That cover up the hardships
Beat into this heart of mine
Like a pretty piece of paper
With a flat line
Masking the painful thorns
Like flowers on a vine

Those flowers will remain
Though through the seasons
They will always change
'Til one day they've had enough
God calls 'em back under
Where they stood through life so tough

Well done, flowers on the vine
Yielding fruit all your life
Despite being weathered
You flowers on the vine

Seeking A New Normal

Frozen in Fear

Finding Joy Again (9/1/18)

I have learned these what ifs take up too much mind space and for each what if (bad thing), I should say also a what if (good thing). Reframe the sorrow and sadness. Find that joy again through the sorrow with the hope in eternal life.

My womb was robbed again
Of the heart that throbbed within
By chance both babies were lost
One in summer and one in winters frost

I'd be lying if I didn't say
Fear now stands in my way
Once more, I said yes to the Lord
But I struggle to truly trust the Word

All the what ifs come to mind
For now two babies, I've left behind
I fear what trials will come next
It's plaguing me, my heart is vexed

I worry for loss of more earthly loves
That they'll be given and taken by Above
Satan has robbed me of innocence and joy
When I used to be excited for girl or boy

I used to look forward to each time
Pregnancy used to be so sublime
But now I want to protect my heart
And fear is where I start

All innocence and joy is gone
Replaced with worry of being left alone
When once there used to be
A seemingly happy tiny inside of me

Overcome by the pain of loss
Too heavy the weight of this cross
I stumble and once more fall
I sink in the water from fear of His call

The devil has shown his face
It's time that prayer took his place
To once more through sorrow employ
That hope which leads to joy

The Postnatal Checkup (10/15/18)

I sit here alone in this room
The light shining down on me
I think of my haunting doom
I'm not what the light wants me to be

I've sat here many times before
Wearing a smile on my face
Waiting for the doc to walk through the door
I didn't used to dread this place

But then you left too soon
I sit motionless and stare
Your heav'nly gain my boon
My heart and arms stripped bare

I don't feed you as I wait
I can't show you to ev'ryone
I don't look forward to a date
When I should expect you come

Nothin' could save you here
I know it wasn't meant to be
I wipe another tear
And still wish you here with me

More thoughts go through my head
My sorrow and fear increase
Two in a row are dead
How can my fears release

How we wished you to stay
Though that wasn't God's will
Can't keep these dreams at bay
We hoped to hold you, still

We dream of what the future holds
We may tread where we fear to go
We may once more be bold
We may rise from our low

Our innocence and joy have died
We are no longer at ease
Where once peace resided
Fear and anxiety be

A deep breath I fake
I can't let it go away
Exhale and leave you in the wake
I can't, I want you to stay

Doctor enters the room
The last time for a while
We talk of prayer and gloom
I leave with a teary smile

I walk out feeling lost
Like you should be with me
Now we know the cost
These two babes in our mem'ry

No more appointments to celebrate
No more heartbeats to hear
But those lives which we did co-create
Remain forever dear

Seeking Sanity

What Happens Next (8/24/18)

After Confession tonight, I knelt in front of the Tabernacle, doing my penance and praying for His Help through this life after loss. I felt lost, more so than after Marky. I thought one loss is all I would have to experience. When the second miscarriage happened, and after the burial, it was harder to muddle through.

Everyone's moved on
The hype is gone
I'm left now on my own
To handle the seeds I've sewn

Seeds of grief continue to grow
 Unsure of the direction to go
The stage of shock has passed
The rest has hit me fast

I write some feelings down
There's no getting around
The heaviness in my heart
Reluctant to depart

Here I go again
Wishing I knew exactly when
I'd get through these emotions within
Be done carrying this burden

When will I be ready to start anew
To taste the morning dew
And once more begin to trust
God's will for all of us

Looking at the Tabernacle tonight
I beg to not lose sight
The words come to me as I stare
And so I utter a humble prayer

Lord may Your grace replace my fear
Help me release all I hold dear
These saints were never mine
They've always been and always will be thine

The Storm (8/24/18)

I had just gotten better after Marky. I had arrived at a place where I could function well again. We found out we were pregnant the day before Independence Day. Then on August 5th, something felt wrong. My morning sickness suddenly stopped. I went into the ER; Lucy's heartbeat was slowing. The next day, she was gone. And so began the process of mourning again. I returned to where I was just a few months prior. She was born via d & c on August 15, buried two days later, exactly 7 months since her brother was buried. I had to weather the storm all over again..

Just when I finished
Putting pieces back together
That's when I
Fell back under the weather
The storm rolls back in
Wind picks up again
The clouds turn black and then
The rain in torrents falls
In pieces of my heart

This storm is like no other
Lightning flashes behind life's curtain
Arises from the aching heart of a mother
Her heart is hidden, but it's hurtin'
No one knows just how much
Can't be uncovered with a touch
But even so, don't rush
She'll not heal for good
Can never be the same again

This storm will rage on its own time
Pain ebbs and flows with the tide
It's course changes on a dime
I'm just along for the ride
No idea where I'll be each day
I have no say
Can't direct the way
This silent storm
Will go

So just sit here with me
Let me weather its path
Just sit and let me be
Help me endure its wrath
Understand I can't tame

The mother is not to blame
I'll never be the same
My innocence is gone
Since the storm came along

Restless Heart (12/10/18)

On this restless night, when I was having trouble falling asleep, I realized I have forgotten again that I have not let my heart rest in Him, and so it remained restless.

Beating away
Every day
My restless heart
Breaks apart

If it didn't love
Like the One above
It wouldn't hurt so
Woulda healed forever ago

It only breaks
For their sakes
If they weren't gone
It'd move on

Worn down heart beats along
To the tune of a different song
Unfamiliar words appear
Heart follows them without fear

Restless my heart this morning
Tries to beat the pain by scorning
It won't forget these losses
Insists I keep these crosses

I can't close my eyes,
I write this time and realize
He wishes me to use this burden
To grow closer to Him, I'm learnin'

Wearing out from my weakness
Without Him, I can't do this
My heart's walls wearing thin
I know it's restless til in Him

Out of control (1/8/19)

You were once on top of the world, unable to be shaken or broken. Then it happens and you're brought to your knees. You're out of control. You try to regain your ability to live, but realize without His Help, it's impossible. He brings you to your knees, where you remember to pray for His help. This thought comes to you as you're spiraling out of control.

Just when I thought
I could handle it well
Another hit blindsided me
And once more I fell

Just when I thought
It wouldn't get worse
One more emotion put
My heart in a hearse

The person is frail
We aren't unbreakable
Our lives derail
This is unshakeable

Now I carry this cross
In the depths of my soul
After my loss
I spiral out of control

I was on top of the world
Thought I had it all together
Throw me any storm
And I could always weather

Thought I was so strong
Thought I couldn't be broken
Turns out all along
I had misspoken

The person is frail
We aren't unbreakable
Our lives derail
This is unshakeable
Now I carry this cross
In the depths of my soul
After my loss

I spiral out of control
We aren't all we need
There's always Another
In times like these we learn to lean
On our Lord and His Mother
Without Him, we are frail

We aren't unbreakable
Our lives will derail
This is unshakeable
But unite our lives to His cross
love Him from depths of my soul
Lay at His feet our earthly loss
Lest we spiral out of control

Make Me New (6/10/19)

After my partial molar pregnancy with Lucy, my body wasn't the same. I kept thinking I was pregnant based on the signs it used to give me when I was, but the tests were all negative. I just want to be myself again, to not have any issues like this.

Lord take away this anguish and pain
Remove my burning desire
To have a little one within me remain
Lord, extinguish this relentless fire

What's going on inside
Where I wish for one to be
Where a little speck wouldst reside
But this time around hath again refused me

Hold my tears for my heart
Let them water my path that lies ahead
Make them glue that doesn't let me fall apart
Grow flowers and life in their stead

Take, o Lord, and make me new
Lead me through this lonely place
For I know not what to do
My trials alone I cannot face

Take my hand
I give You the lead
You help me stand
And know what I need

Each time I learn
What I already know
If Your help I spurn
I give the battle to the foe

In my weakness
I continue to fall
I accept my meekness
I return Your call

So Take, o Lord, and make me new
My trials alone I cannot face
I know not what to do
Lead me through this lonely place

My Heart Needs A Break (10/6/19)

I've learned it's ok to take a break. Don't expect yourself to be the same as before. It's ok to rest a while from what once brought a smile. Let God heal your heart

Say I'm not who
I used to be
And what I do
Now won't set me free
My heart just needs to
Reset its rhythm
And I'll find my
Beat once more within

It's not that I
Don't have what it takes
There just came a point when
I needed to make
Time for my heart
To catch a break

There are times when I stand
My back against the wall
Realize that day
I still feel so small
Weakness courses through me
My strength fails again
God reaches for me
Outstretched merciful Hand

He gives me
All that it takes
When I reach the point
I need to make
Time for my heart
To catch a break

Heart pumps life through me
In vain tries to revive
I see how I need Him
To keep me alive

He gives me
All that it takes
When I reach the point
I need to make
Time for my heart
To catch a break

Challenges of Change

Vicious Cycle (11/22/18)

Just in the moment when I feel I'm moving forward, something is there to remind me and I'm set back to where I was before, as if to start the process over again. It makes me wonder if I ever as far along as I thought I was in the healing process. Or was I wishing? Regardless, sometimes it takes a vicious cycle to remind us where we truly are, to sit with ourselves in those moments, to truly feel it, and not to attempt to hurry it along.

Come outside of myself
Put my heart on the shelf
Start to come alive
Trying my best to thrive

Something holds me back
There are pieces of me I lack
Something stuck inside
I'm just along for the ride

These days, I can't retrieve
When the present now leaves
When the future becomes the past
And life passes by too fast

I feel this illness squandering
Leaves me constantly wandering
Wishing I could myself heal
Make my heart different feel

Slipping out of my control
Happiness my sadness stole
Years wear down my face
My youthfulness, pain's replaced

No longer complacent and sublime
Worn down by passing time
Faking it doesn't work anymore
I face the future I have in store

Can't just make it on my own
Learned I can't do it on my own
This life continues to make me humble
My pride makes me stumble

Each time a stone is cast
Mistaken that it's the last
Puts me on a different path
Avoiding my life's wrath

Tryin so hard to join the rest
Failing each day to pass the test
Wanting so badly to see
That person I used to be

Struggling to let the light come in
Awaiting new life to begin
Thinking doing so would be wrong
Aren't I supposed to just be strong?

Keep the bad inside
Til this storm subside
Why does this take so long?
This is where I don't belong

It's where I always thought
I'd never allow myself to be caught
I do well and think grief is through
Then something makes me think of you

It takes me back to then
And I start all over again
I remember I can't lose my heart
And I go back to where I started

And like a habitual sin
I return to what's going on within
Whenever I try to move on
I remember you both are gone

What fueled my drive on this road
I can't seem to unload
Every time I think I'm done
I remember you, little ones

Leave It Behind (11/26/18)

I wish to snap out of it, out of this reality, as if it's not really mine. It's so hard to keep thinking I can just return to life as it was and leave this nightmare behind.

Want to laugh
Want to smile
It's been forced
For a while

It felt genuine
For the first time
My body in harmony but
All changed on a dime

I stop and remember
The memories that hold me back
Fearing I'll forget them
If I shed the mourning black

Each day
I struggle to find
The courage to just
Leave it all behind

Feels like I'm
Living on a different earth
Never recovered from
Shock after their births

Goin through the motions
Every single day
I think I'm coming back
But I'm still drifting away

Reality so different
Living each moment on the outside
Wishing so much to be within
But can only sit tight and ride by

These ties hold me back
Can't stop wishing to unbind
Loose the ropes
And leave it all behind

I wish to return to
All that I enjoyed before
But I find myself waiting behind

That door closed forevermore
It still remains that nothing has changed
Despite my hopes to
Have emotions rearranged

No matter the situation
And regardless of all I have here
All I can think of is
Who I have lost, and my ensuing fear

Can't seem to loose
The chains that bind
Eager, but hesitant, to
Leave it all behind

Moving Forward to Normal (12/8/18)

This day was the last of my weekly hCG testing after Lucy. I had 6 months of monthly testing remaining. I kept waiting to shift gears, to be happy again now that my numbers were normal. I kept thinking my new normal began then. No, my new normal began back after losing them. That new normal is constituted by living a better life, in hopes of reaching Heaven where they dwell, not just to be with them, for their job as saints is to lead us to He, who created us. And so I live for THAT.

Driving home from the hospital
For the last time
Got my good results
No tears in my eyes

Couldn't release my emotions
No, I couldn't cry
Never able to let the tears fall
No matter how hard I try

As I thought
I continued to drive
All will expect me
To happily move on with life

You got what you needed
Your spirits should be high
You're healthy again
Your sorrows should be nigh

Stopped the car before making a turn
And I realize
As I sit here stuck
Time continues to fly

The light changed
And so did I
I headed home
Still stopped up inside

With the new understanding
This is what it's like
New normal isn't a destination
But the constant flux that is my life

Lost Sheep, Lost Sleep (12/10/18)

Oh, my little saints! You remind me that comforts of this earth aren't what will lead us to heaven, but rather what we do when those comforts are taken from us, even the comfort of sleep. I know this, yet still in the dark and lonesome night, I sometimes forget to invoke you to call upon Him to aid me.

Leave the year behind
You remain on my mind
Though we are far apart
You're imprinted on my heart

For my two departed sheep
I lose sleep
Like a good shepherd
Missing some of his herd

Can't breathe you away
Try as I may
You're still stuck inside
Left a hole, deep and wide

I spend the night
Putting up a fight
You won't fill up
My empty cup

Trying to sleep
Can't count lost sheep
The reference is too strong
This night, too long

Though blankets are warm
My heart won't conform
That emptiness is cold
Though the night be old

So how can I deal
When you continue to steal
My sleep on earth
Reminding me of your sleep at birth

Words Stuck in Grief (12/14/18)

It's so often difficult to find a way to put to words all the emotions that are bottled up inside.

Through muddled mind
I struggle to find
The words that have
My heart in a bind

All that I feel
My joy they steal
And from clarity
My verbiage seems to reel

I write and then stop
As if chased by a cop
As I run out of gas
Driving up a mountain top

Grief is the exhaust
That makes me feel so lost
Emotions like vapor
From the tailpipe are tossed

My mind rushes fast
Like the mile markers passed
'Til one night
It runs out of gas

It finally rests at ease
Finds a moments peace
When the words held hostage
Find their release

A New Life (1/2/19)

A year since my last appt hearing Marky's heartbeat, and I'm certain a year since he died. He didn't grow after that date and hormone levels had dropped to pre-pregnancy levels. I held out hope and tried to help, but it wasn't to be so. And since then, I've been living a new life.

It's been a year
And you're still not here
Not on this earth
My little saint Marky, dear
My heart beats fast
Though the day's gone past
Though you weren't gone
I knew something was wrong
You moved on the screen
But that was just like TV
We know how those shows end
People all pretend
The actors all in place
Put on a poker face
Hiding what is real
And how they truly feel
At the end of the show
Back to reality they go
Imprints they depart
On every viewer's heart

And on the last call
Main character and sidekick fall
So that show ends
But it's sequel begins
Show must go on
Though the pride and joy be gone
One character most affected
Others lead the new life expected
The one must still play her part
With the hole in her heart
Like a hero keeping up the fight
She goes along with this bittersweet new life

At Odds with Myself (1/29/19)

I can feel my arms weighted down by the tears I wish I could let out, by feelings I don't even try to suppress, but which remain below the surface, nonetheless. It seems I'm at an impasse with myself, wishing to move on, but can't stop remembering they're gone.

Empty arms reminded they're holding nothing again
Hurting heart beating the pain away within
Wrestling the tears still stuck inside
Wishing those tears I could cry

Listen to my body tell me what it needs
While I fight to be my former me
It's only natural to resist
The uncomfortable changes that come with this

Can't turn away forever
I hear myself say never
Then I take the fall
I try to resist the call

Feel the weight of tears brimming at my shoulders
Wishing my internal fire they would smolder
Release all that's weighing me down and burning hot
The feelings stubbornly stay like an unwanted forget me not

As if these feelings I wish not to suppress
Remain below the surface nonetheless
Wishing isn't enough to propel me to move on
When every ounce of myself remembers that you're gone

I try to somehow make a start
But it's the blind leading the blind in the dark
How does my mind lead the rest?
To take flight from this familiar nest

When all I wish to do
Is remain still, remembering you
When everyone else is gone
And can't understand why I'm not done

In a world that moves so fast
Like the time since you passed
A mother's heart wants nothin more than to stay
But the world wants its own way

Like those two outside forces are at odds
So, too, my mind and body fights what is God's
How hard is it to let go of what I want for me?
And in my darkest night to let Him take the lead

Why do I know all these things?
Yet refuse to flow with whatever life brings
My heart at odds as it refuses to let go of what it knows
Of the memories it wishes to keep close

This is part of the new normal and I must
Allow myself to adjust
Work on understanding what is God's
And let go of what's keeping me at odds

Put You to Rest (4/3/19)

You were due
The middle of June
I went through
Losing you
Broken heart
Worlds apart
Through the trials and pains
True Joy forever reigns
So with a sober face
And a veil with black lace
God gave me you as a test
And I laid you to rest

In my head I was
Preparing just because
I was ready for you to be
In this place where I could see
And hold you close
Instead I'm morose
Saw the ground and the hole
Priest said the sacred words of burial
I watched your tiny box lowered down
Denial couldn't muster a frown
I tried my very best
Watched as they laid you to rest

Spent the next many days
Wishing for words no one says
You can't return from where you've gone
So I'm here left to move on
No one knows the turmoil inside
No one hops on my lonely ride
This cross only I can bear
A strong arm they won't spare

On Christ alone I rely
To hold my tears while I cry
You're Home at His behest
Here on earth I laid you to rest
Slowly working through my tears
Battling all my earthly fears

Doing what's best for me
All the while refusing to see
I'm not standing here alone
Doesn't mean I pick up the phone
God's Spirit is on a different line
He's been trying to reach out to mine
I've been deaf this entire time
But life changed on a dime
When I let my worries leave their nest
And I let Him put them to rest
So I continue on life's walk
Keep talking the talk
With sorrow nipping my heels
Occasionally visited by my feels
Knowing it's okay to let them out
But they're not what life's about
I can hold you close while moving on
You're still here even though you're gone
I don't have to let go
I'm allowed to have a high and low
I can still have days it's hard to get dressed
You remain though I've laid you to rest

How Miscarriages Affect Relationships

Beauty from the Pain (10/27/18)

I tend to have a difficult time speaking about my hurt on this journey and find it easier to share my words written down. From this pain I feel, comes beauty through words, which, when spoken, might not come out as well. Sometimes, we need other methods of sharing how we feel, something other than speaking, and that is ok. Let the beauty flow from the pain.

Write it out
Share your doubt
Hesitate a minute
Is your heart truly in it
Do you really believe
Others will see what you perceive
Will they look past the words
And understand your hurt
That this is your way
Pain leaves through words you say
You're trying to make your return
Prayin' you're not spurned
You try and cleave
Praying they don't leave
They're your sanity this moment
Comfort as you lament
Tears fall and land below
On the seed ready to grow
Let it out and give it room
For from your hurt, beauty blooms

This Is Life (12/10/18)

I would be remiss if I said marriage was easy at any point, but it might be especially hard following loss. Sometimes spouses are just on different pages, sometimes their grief doesn't match up. But I'm reminded of our vows and how they didn't say we were there for each other only during the positive, but also for the trials, the sorrow, the rough and tough. For this is what true love is. This is how we imitate Christ's love as best we can. THIS is life.

I don't wanna Monday
It's not a fun day
But I'm a fan of Sunday night
With Argentina red wine
Relaxin' with a good time
Everything's feeling just right

Sitting here with you
Watching football on the tube
Watched my team pull through today
Goin to bed, where it feels like I just was
Then it's morning again just because
Doin the week again, if I must,
It'll be okay

This is life
With husband, with wife
Every day begins
And those days end
We make it what we can
'Cause all we have is this life

We become mom and dad
The good comes with the bad
We take it cuz it's all we have been given
God's blessings are ours
Even in our darkest hours
The seeds grow into flowers from Heav'n

Through thick and thin
God helps us win
From when we begin til death
Each day learning to love you more
Findin' windows after closed doors
You're who I breathe for til my last breath

This is life
With husband, with wife
Every day begins
And those days end
So we make it what we can
'Cause all we have is this life

This is the life we have
We have to give it back
All that matters in the end
Ain't the things we get, but the love we send

This is life
With husband, with wife
Every day begins
And those days end
So we make it what we can
'Cause all we have is this life

Moving Through the Silence (1/6/19)

Often times, when women suffer a miscarriage or pregnancy loss, she isn't sure who to talk to. Some people may be more open to listening and inducing conversation, helping mom to open up, while others aren't sure of what to say. So many times, it is the case we just continue on, thinking about our babies and the emotions that follow loss. Daily we just move through the silence.

My head pounds loudly
Thoughts of them run through
I honor them proudly
As any mom would do
Go through my day
Thinking as I move through each task
I speak what I wish to say
If only you ask
Catering to my heart's defiance
By otherwise not speaking at all
Moving through the silence
And talking to the wall
I long to speak their names
And of their lives as well
I know it seems quite lame
But I desire their stories to tell
For with the beauty of their mem'ry arises
A testimony to their lives
Only when I move outside the silence
Of all I keep inside

When You Feel Like Letting Go (2/27/19)

I know firsthand how miscarriage can lead to feeling in a completely different world than your spouse. No one understands it as you do and many times, it feels like you're ready to let go, but that's when the test of love is given...hanging on when you feel like letting go...when you feel like that's where you're being led, look to Christ's example. His love is always holding on even when it feels like He's letting go or we feel like letting go. So I've been hanging on to the hem of His garment even when I feel like letting go.

Got married and
All was goin' well
Could they stand the test
Only time would tell
On the surface
Everything seemed fine
But when push came to shove
They walked a fine line

It was then that
They learned it wasn't about
Giving up when you
Are clouded by every doubt
When it seemed like they were done
She learned all she needed to know
Love is hangin' on when ya
Feel like lettin' go

He hung on the cross after
Being beaten and derided
They scowled and cursed
And His teachings they all Chided
He could have shaken the dust
And could have given up on us all
But he continued on
Rising after each painful fall

Look to Him and
We see what it's all about
He gave up His life
Erased every doubt
Through Him we learned
The true meaning of what we should know
Because of Love, He hung on that Cross
When it'd have been so easy to let go

On this earth and in this time
We follow the worldly road
Which teaches us to stray from the
Way He followed
Lose our memory and
We stray from what we know
His Love reminds us to hang on
When we feel like lettin' go

Hangin' on through the hurt
Caused by our sins
The pain He feels
When we refuse to let Him in
The mercy He has
When waves of life toss us to and fro
He holds us with His Love even
When we feel like He's lettin' go

His true love is hangin on when
We think He's lettin' go

Standin' Sideways (9/6/19)

Spending my days chasin' parked cars
In a dead end parking lot
In my race against time on this earth
Battle with life to heal my scars
Trying to give everything all I've got
To get it all done before I die since birth

But it seems like
Things don't go right
With my plans for the day
I think I'm climbin'
Defeating my mountain
Turns out I'm just standing sideways

We said our vows
Thought we'd figure out
How to handle the good and the bad
It was harder to do
And harder to prove
When the tough times hit with the sad

We both just stood tight
When things didn't go right
With our plans for those days
We thought we were climbin'
Makin it up that mountain
Turned out we were just standing sideways

Turned away when we couldn't find words
Found out silence cut deeper than swords

We needed to hold each other tight
When moments don't turn out right
With our plans any given day
When we think we're climbin'
Makin it up life's mountain
Find out we're just standing sideways

Hidden Behind A Smile (9/9/19)

Cold and distant
No one gets it
Just pin it all on me
Move on from the past
The present can't last
And no one cares to see

But a heart breaks In the silence
And no one hears or sees
It will be a little while
'Cause it's hidden behind a smile
And weary fallen knees

This is somethin' that
Stays around
Live with this through life
Can't beat it into the ground
This is more than
Just a feeling
Somethin' happened
Sent me reeling

My heart broke In the silence
But no one hears or sees
And it will be a little while
'Cause it's hidden behind a smile
And weary fallen knees

So look beyond the beauty for the pain
Look into my eyes for the hidden rain

Hold me here in the silence
Now that you can see
And It may take a little while
To raise me off my weary fallen knees
As you uncover what's behind my hidden smile

Hope in Healing

Love's Sacrifice (9/30/18)

Written for the month of October, Pregnancy and Infancy Loss Awareness month.

This month we remember you all
Whose parents loved and took the fall
Who lost an earthly joy
To heavens gain did employ

Our fiat was full of love
Sacrifice mirroring His, Above
The gift of self, truly given
By Covenant with God were we driven

Our love through life hath shone
And yet we feel alone
For daily prayer, they show our face
Helping us find Love's embrace

As we struggle with every step to heal
And slowly somewhat better feel
We, who find our joys to be sober
As we enter this month, October

We are reminded daily of His off'ring
As we remember our saintly offspring
This earthly purgatory isn't for naught
These hellish flames aren't so hot

We think of our ultimate desire
And suddenly our drives quench the fire
We remember to Whom we shall return
And once more, joy within does burn

For pregnancy loss (10/2/18)

Remember, you are never alone. Even in the moments when it seems like no one cares, no one understands, no one grasps your individual and unique pain, nor can they help you bear this cross you carry, you are not alone. Our Lord walks with you always. He has gone before you with the suffering of loss. Lean on Him, ask His help. He will not forsake you.

You walk now as our Lady has done
With similar grief as when she lost her Son
May our Lord show His Mercy
And May in Heaven your child be
To constantly pray for God's Grace
That you may be wrapped in His embrace
I know you feel your child's presence forever
The bond of mother and baby never sever
Though you carry forever grief of loss
We are here to help carry your cross
May you know you walk not by yourself
For we are all here to pray and to help

A Mother's Loss (11/29/18)

Losing a baby is not easy, regardless of how far along you are or if baby has been born already.
Yet, when we suffer loss, and although we feel such heavy sorrow within our hearts, it is important to offer up our sufferings, as Christ so did for us on the Cross, as Mary did when she suffered a Mother's loss.

Daily, I encounter my earthly pain
And take up my life's cross
I think of the heavenly gain
Through A mother's loss

It's one thing that keeps me going
My heart is weak, yet the beat is strong
My lungs, life's air keep blowing
Keeps leading me Where I belong

On this path, I trudge on blind
Struggling to hear His Word
Fighting thoughts within my mind
So his Truth might be heard

Unite my troubles to His
He knows how to carry a Cross
What my weakness forbids
He rectifies with His loss
He leads us to Heaven
As we suffer here on earth
Take trials we're given
He gives us Joyful berth

To our hearts torment we surrender
With ev'ry beat we feel
What true love's hurt must render
To obtain Heaven's final seal

So, help me suffer wisely
Through these and all things gone
To know just what precisely
I must do til My earthly life is done

As I suffer through earthly pain
And take up my daily cross
Lead me to focus on His gain
Through His Mother's loss

Christmas Hope (12/14/18)

Despite the pain of not having them here, it remains important through sorrow to hope, and so we shall have joy. On Christmas, Our Lady knew there would be sorrow to come, yet she remained joyful because she had hope. May we all be like her and maintain that undying hope through all trials life throws our way. We aren't living for the joys and comforts of this world, but of the Next.

The Star will shine its heavenly bright
The Son will come to joyful tears
All is quiet on this silent night
Hushed for a moment are all fears

So is the picture I see for the future
Something to happen in coming years
Please come home for Christmas, a cure
A plea fallen on deafened ears

No one here can bring you
Home is a different Place
Nothing left for me to do
Pray to feel Heav'ns embrace

For this moment in earthly time
Through the sorrows I feel
Keep Christ's journey in mind
And know someday I'll heal

But hope won't bring you back
Sighing won't fulfill me anymore
That fleeting happiness I lack
Won't prepare me for what's in store

I've loved and lost, but still carry hope
For the One who came to dwell within
His life was announced on joyous note
And then in sorrow, died for all sin

So amidst the sorrow
And the painful route I've been
There's hope for tomorrow
That I might join them once again

My Loss for Your Glory (12/23/18)

I mourn here for earthly loss amidst earthly comfort, yet you had nothing. Help me to be poor and not rely on earthly things, but to be rich in spirit, for there is where I will find consolation. And it is how I will draw closer to Thee. May my losses be always for Your Glory.

I wear the necklace with your names
I carry it with pride
You're with me through life's games
You're along for the ride

May the memory of time with you
Bring me happiness and peace
And May the Lord carry me through
The loneliness that's grief's beast

Reflecting on the Holy Family
And the things which they had not
Realize I handle my riches poorly
Yet, they rejoiced in what they got

A manger for His bed
Entered the world one cold eve
Laid where the livestock all fed
Yet in worldly comfort, I sit and grieve

My saints, with your prayers
All my things, give to our Lord
And from my sorrows' layers
Bring solace from th'Incarnate Word

Unfold my pains in life
Use them for the Will of Thee
Help me as mom and wife
Give of myself through difficulty

You put me on this earth
Not to be evils slave
But to love and serve you from birth
Not to the devil's way shall I cave

From the dark of my human sight,
Set me free
So only for Your True Light,
Do I have eyes to see

(12/28/18)

...ı year. So many times, I've felt alone, but that's ...nanness. The times I've opened my heart and ......u to allow God and His Mercy and Graces in are the times I've been at peace and surrounded by His Love, which is enough for me.

A year has come and gone
The world has continued to move on
While I remain stuck like before
Behind a closed and stubborn door
So now I can't operate, or so I feel
Since no one understands my pain is real
It's in moments like these I must
Pray to the One Who is Merciful and Just
It is He Who understands
He, better than any man
He Who has endured pain unlike another
And she who witnessed, Mary, His Mother
In lonely moments like these
Reflect on Their pains for mine to cease
For this is my path to holiness taken
Know, my heart, He hath not forsaken
I am never alone as it seems
Though this isn't the life of my dreams
Happiness in this life is fleeting
True happiness is found in Heaven's greeting
So waste not my searching on earthly goods
Seek those of Heaven as I should
It is then that all will be well
And the Peace of the Lord in me shall dwell
This is when I realize that though they're gone
With our Lord and all of Heaven, I'm not alone

With a Song (12/31/18)

Although writing has been my catharsis, it merely serves as a release of present emotions, not their memories. Those I will carry with me always. This is my journey to hope from despair.

Two months ago
Seems so far away
I definitely know
How hard you pray

No matter how hard I try
I keep trying to fight
Regardless of the tears I cry
With every word I write

Timidly I step
Can't right what feels so wrong
I walk slowly as time has crept
Can't write your memory away with a song

My feet find ground once more
And with some courage they tread
The second time adventure lures
Though I cling to safety's thread

Emerge from my shell on a dare
Follow Jesus' lead
He pulls me from the devil's snare
From these bonds I'm freed

Holding on To Nothing (1/18/19)

Holding on to the nothing that I have of Marky and Lucy. As if their memories are something more than just memories, something tangible like I keep thinking will return if I wish hard enough. But each time, they remain only that. Memories.

I think with each day
That passes me by
I wish you'd have stayed
But it was your time to die

I realize it was your turn to go
To that Place we all desire
Even though this I know
My heart remains on its pyre

My faith may be the size
Of a mustard seed
At least, I hope in His Eyes
He sees I'm giving Him the lead

I understand more deeply now
All life is in His grasp
Yet still I wonder why and how
To my saints memories I clasp

I keep wishing it were real
The tangible part of them that was
I know it's only what I hope to feel
As any grieving mother does

But I know so long as I
Keep thinking I'll find something
Instead of being filled with Heavenly Light
I'll be empty holding onto nothing

Transfigured Soul (5/26/19)

Took a couple chances
We shouldn't have
Because of the babies
We couldn't have
Two weeks later I was
Seein' lines all over the place
Turns out they were
Just reflections of my face
Hoping against hope
For what I wouldn't get
Tryin' to understand and embrace
God sayin' not yet
Hard to trust there'll ever
Be any more
Despair sinkin in and feelin
Like God closed that door
People tell me
Not to dwell
But how do you escape
That kinda hell

When they say that
I'm so young
Can't help but think they
Should just bite their tongue
They don't feel the emptiness
I have inside
That comes and goes like
The ebb and flow of the tide
Where the only thing now
Taking up space
Is my longing to
Carry another face
Where my two saints
Used to be
A lonely hole
Untouched inside of me
I keep reaching for a
Seemingly unattainable goal
Every time I get close,
God transfigures my soul

Modern Day Job (6/10/19)

When it feels like everything is not working out in your favor, keep the hope like a modern-day Job.

Sittin with the kids
At the car dealer this morn
I pass by the adults
In the room next door
See a lady at a table
By the front desk
Gettin' her nails did
They're gonna look the best

Keep the hope
Modern day Job

Lost two babies
They left earth last year
Wanna have more
But I have much to fear
Friends have positive pregnancy tests
I can't help but feel left out and beat
As if this is a race
And I'm meeting defeat

Don't lose hope
Modern day Job

My stomach aches
I ponder what's goin on inside me
My heart breaks
Why am I not where I wish to be
I try to surrender it all to God
But like every day that's passed
And every time I'm told to give it up
It's just like the last

I cling to hope
Like a modern day Job

Another negative test
One more blood draw nears
I ponder if I'll ever have more
Surrounded by those fears
An anniversary approaches
Reminds me once again
Of who I lost and wish were here
Reminds me what would have been
Hope begs me to stay
Modern day Job

Mama (6/22/19)

Driving on the way to moms' night out last Thursday, I saw cumulus clouds with a hole that had the sunlight shining through. I had been thinking a lot about Marky since his due date anniversary had just passed. It'd been a hard week. The light was as if he was trying to tell me something...

See the clouds in the sky
With the sun peeking through
That's me, mama
Talkin to you
Peering through the darkness
That little light
Is me, mama
Watchin tonight

I know you miss me, mama
I know you long to hold me close
I see you desperately,
Wishing you could count my toes
I'm watchin' for ya, mama
When you get to the end of your road
It's me mama, waitin' for you

I left a little early
Sorry I left you alone
God called, mama
So I had to go
He gave me to you and
I made you smile
Don't worry, mama
It's only a while

I know you miss me, mama
I know you long to hold me close
I see you desperately,
Wishing you could count my toes
I'm watching for ya, mama

When you get to the end of your road
I'm here mama, waitin' for you

Even though we're so far apart
I'm always alive in your heart
Though you miss me, mama and
Though you long to hold me close
I'm here prayin' for ya, mama
Through your highs and lows
I'll be waitin for ya, mama
When you reach the end of your road
No rush mama, I'm waitin' for you
Yeah, It's me mama, waitin' for you
All things new again (8/12/19)

You win some, you lose some others
Some ya keep, some are gone forever
Yet you're still expected to move on
Keep goin' after they're gone

Just when I think I
Can't carry on
Past the memory of
My two who are gone
He comes through again
Making all things new again

Goin through the motion
Riding the waves of this ocean
Knowing God will take all suffering
While life seems to be buffering

Makes me think I
Can't carry on
Past the memory of
My two who are gone
He comes through again
Making all things new again

I'm learnin' to seek
Him whenever I'm weak

For I know He can
Help me carry on
While I hold onto the memories of
My two who are gone
He comes through just when
I need Him to make all things new again

Look Up (10/4/19)

Sometimes life gets in the way
No one knows what to say
You start panicking
Looking frantically
For a lifeline here
Well I'm here
To tell you

When you're feeling down
And you need some help
Don't turn a frown
Look up
Don't turn around
You won't get anywhere new
Don't gaze at the ground
No, just look up

When you run into a wall
And it disrupts your day
Tempted to just fall
And throw it all away
When hard times get in the way
All I've gotta say
Is look up

When you're feeling down
And you need some help
Don't look around
Look up
Don't turn a frown
You won't get anywhere new
Don't gaze at the ground

No, just look up
All you need is beyond the sky
You'll find it all when you
Gaze in His eyes

So look up
When you're feeling down
And you need some help
Don't look around
Look up
Don't turn a frown
You won't get anywhere new
Don't gaze at the ground
No, just look up

Your Direction (10/12/19)

Finding myself once more with a hole in my soul, yearning to fill it and I know once more, it's only by seeking Him that my heart can ever rest. He fills me up with all I need.

I go weak in the knees
But I suppose that's good
Drop 'em to the floor
Like I know I should
Just a little more
Than I ever would

I'm in ruins here
But You build me high
Folding my hands
Reach to the sky
You make demands

But they lead to eternal life
And here I am
Takin another step in the right direction
There I go
Moving forward with Your blessin'
All because I looked to You
And with Love and Affection
You led me forward in Your direction

So, where does this leave me now
When I hit another fork in the road
Bade me to follow with hope
The path You once showed
That's how to cope
With this pain I have stowed

And here I am again
Takin another step in the right direction
There I go once more
Moving forward with Your blessin'
All because I looked to You
And with Love and Affection
You led me forward in Your direction

You're there to remind me
To follow Your directions
Lead me once more
With the Grace from Your blessin
'When I but turn to You
Seeking your Love and Affection
You lead me in
Your direction

The End